WARNER MEMORIAL LIBRARY
EASTERN COLLEGE
ST. DAVIDS, PA. 19087

Confronting Drug Abuse

CONTRIBUTORS

Andrew A. Sorensen

Assistant professor, College of Human Ecology, Cornell University, Ithaca, New York, member of Cornell University Drug Education Committee. B.A., University of Illinois, M.P.H., University of Michigan, B.D., M. Phil., Ph.D., Yale University.

Gerald D. Klee

Staff psychiatrist, Sinai Hospital, Baltimore, Maryland. Previously professor of psychiatry, Temple University School of Medicine, Philadelphia. Undergraduate education, Princeton and McGill Universities, M.D., Harvard Medical School.

T. Guthrie Speers, Jr.

Minister, The First Presbyterian Church, New Canaan, Connecticut. B.A., Princeton University, B.D., Union Theological Seminary.

Henry S. G. Cutter

Research psychologist, Veterans Administration Hospital, Brockton, Massachusetts, research associate, department of psychology, Boston University. B.A., Harvard College, Ph.D., Boston University.

Gordon A. Martin, Jr.

Senior Associate in juridical services of Harbridge House, commissioner of the Massachusetts Commission Against Discrimination, chairman of the Boston Coordinating Council on Drug Abuse. From 1961 to 1967, U.S. Department of Justice as trial attorney in Civil Rights Division, and later First Assistant U.S. Attorney for Massachusetts. B.A., Harvard College; J.D., New York University Law School.

Harvey W. Feldman

Assistant professor of sociology, Brandeis University, Waltham, Massachusetts. B.A., New York University, Ph.D., Brandeis University.

David E. Joranson

Administrative assistant to the superintendent of Mendota State Hospital, Madison, Wisconsin, Associate Producer of WHA-TV's "The Drug Problem," chairman of the treatment and rehabilitation section of the Wisconsin Governor's Conference on Drugs and Alcohol. B.A., M.S.W., University of Wisconsin.

CONFRONTING DRUG ABUSE

APPROACHES TO ITS PREVENTION AND TREATMENT

EDITED BY
ANDREW A. SORENSEN

A PILGRIM PRESS BOOK ● PHILADELPHIA

HV
5801
.C6

12/14/82

Copyright © 1972 United Church Press
Library of Congress Catalog Card Number 79-188612
ISBN 0-8298-0233-9

For my parents—
Albert Aaron and Margaret Lindquist Sorensen—
who taught me to care by caring

TABLE OF CONTENTS

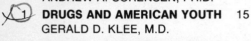

FOREWORD
BY ALLYN B. LEY, M.D.

The fact that the use of drugs has become a pervasive problem in our society has emerged only in the last few years. The problem was always there, of course, though it was separated neatly from the mainstream of social awareness by considering alcoholism as a different sort of problem and narcotic addiction as a problem affecting only a limited segment of society, to be dealt with more by the law than by other social agencies. The increasing use of potent psychopharmacologic agents in medical practice was considered a professional matter, between individual patients and their physicians, with little relevance to "drug abuse" in the epidemiological sense.

As the use of drugs has become widespread ("epidemic") among middle-class youth, we are beginning to appreciate that these formerly segmented problems do indeed have common roots and sometimes direct interrelationships. A son, whose commuter father gets loaded every weekend and whose mother is constantly renewing prescriptions for the tranquilizers offered by her physician, finds it difficult to understand why his particular method of finding solace is so violently condemned. In some ways he feels more closely associated with the narcotic addict in the ghetto than he does with his peers in suburbia.

Now that we all are confronted with drug abuse, we find that each of us brings his own attitudes and preconceptions to the problem. Those of us who work closely with college and university students have quite different views from those who are primarily legally oriented or from those whose experience is mostly among disadvantaged youth. This is to say nothing of the medical profession, which is, by and large, the epitome of the Establishment and paradoxically has seemed to the anti-Establishment youth as the least relevant agency to deal with the social problems of drugs.

The value of this collection of essays is that it is presented by a diverse group. This obviously has its disadvantages in terms of continuity and cohesiveness, but it does collect in one volume the views from different points of vantage of thoughtful people, all deeply concerned with this major societal problem. Even though the details of the problem change rapidly and apparently unpredictably, the basic principles related to usage of drugs remain the same. They are well expressed here by each of the essayists according to his position on the scene.

Allyn B. Ley, M.D.
Director, Cornell University
Health Services

INTRODUCTION
BY ANDREW A. SORENSEN, PH.D.

This collection of essays has been published to enable you to get a broader understanding of some of the reasons for drug abuse in our society. If you are already working with drug programs in your community, perhaps this book will give you new ways of looking at old problems. If you are not yet involved, it suggests many avenues of activity which you might explore in your respective communities.

This book does not pretend to solve the myriad problems related to drug abuse. There are no easy solutions to them. But several concerned and informed persons, each with training and experiences different from the others, have pooled their resources to offer you an unusually comprehensive presentation of the nexus of drug abuse issues.

No single person—or group of persons—has all the answers to the drug problem. But this collection of essays represents a group of people with widely diverse training and experiences—a psychiatrist, a psychologist, a lawyer, a social worker, sociologists, and clergymen—who strongly believe that collectively we can do a better job of suggesting approaches to the drug problem than any one of us individually. As we have collaborated in organizing this book, we hope that you will find ways to collaborate with the people in your respective communities to confront the problem of drug abuse.

Although we give different explanations for the widespread abuse of drugs in our society, we are by no means contradicting one another. Rather, each of us is taking a point of view that he has developed as a result of his professional background and reflection on experiences in actual drug programs. As you read these pages, you will find that looking at the knotty complex of issues we call the drug problem through a number of different but complementary perspectives will help you to understand the problem infinitely better than if you were looking through the eyes of only one person.

In chapter 1, Dr. Klee looks at the youth culture and its propensity for the excessive use of drugs and the psychological impact which such drug use has upon individuals. He then describes the kinds of measures we may take to treat drug abusers and how we, as a society, might respond more adequately to the young people.

In chapter 2, the Rev. Mr. Speers cleverly characterizes the barriers that tend to divide members of the same family and same community from one another. He suggests that tearing down these barriers will not solve the drug problem but will make us more sensitive to the problem and to one another.

In chapter 3, Dr. Cutter, a psychologist, explores the ways in which the attitudes people have about drugs affect the experiences they have with drugs and drug users. He suggests that both drug users and non-users could benefit from close scrutiny of their own attitudes toward drugs.

In chapter 4, Mr. Martin, a lawyer with experience as a law professor, takes a hard look at the relation of our legal and judicial system to drug users. He contends that our drug laws and the manner in which these laws are administered often encourage disrespect for the law, and consequently invite even greater drug abuse. Paradoxically, Mr. Martin notes that, at the same time, the legal and judicial system is becoming more responsive to the provision of treatment for drug offenders.

In chapter 5, Dr. Feldman, a sociologist, relates drug use to community social structure. He examines the use of drugs among adolescents in the context of a peer-group system, and imaginatively describes how this system operates in one community.

In chapter 6, Mr. Joranson, a social worker, argues that our present drug laws are based on moral and legal, rather than scientific definitions of the drug problem. He points out that our drug laws have created new problems without solving the old ones, and urges us to take *all* drug use out of the arena of criminalization before we attempt to treat and control drug abuse.

Chapter 7, "The Crutch That Cripples," is the report of the Committee on Alcoholism and Drug Dependence of the American Medical Association's Council on Mental Health. This report distinguishes the abuse of various kinds of drugs, and offers some valuable suggestions for the treatment and prevention of drug abuse.

In the concluding chapter, I explore the ways in which you can get involved in drug treatment and prevention in your own community. These days, there are many books about drugs; dozens of these books contain numerous charts covered with polysyllabic names of strange (and familiar) drugs, glossaries of slang terms used in the drug culture, and autobiographical sketches of drug addicts. But very rarely is the reader told: here are some courses of action you may take to do something about drug abuse. This concluding chapter attempts to fill that gap.

Without the efforts of the following persons, this book would not have been published: Dr. Emil Rothstein and Dr. Wyatt C. Jones, who assisted in organizing the drug seminar at which earlier versions of three of these papers were presented; Dr. William Winick, director of the Veterans Administration Hospital in Brockton, Massachusetts, who graciously allowed the use of the facilities of that hospital for the seminar; Donna I. Sorensen, who offered many helpful suggestions in editing the papers; and Dorothy Bliss, Andrea Rouse, and Sue Sovocool, who typed much of the manuscript.

CHAPTER 1

DRUGS AND AMERICAN YOUTH

DRUGS AND AMERICAN YOUTH[1]
BY GERALD D. KLEE, M.D.

Youth is a time for exploration. It is a time for experimentation, for change, a time for revolt. The late adolescent and young adult sees the world as though for the first time. He tweaks the noses of his elders and demands to discover the world for himself. He doesn't believe it's the way they say it is, nor that it must be the way that he finds it. He is usually optimistic and idealistic, although he may conceal it behind a facade of cynicism. He demands the exposure of fraud and deceit in all areas of life, the abandonment of all illusions, and the establishment of a new social order based upon love and other noble sentiments and principles.

What I have described has always been an aspect of this period of life. While it may lead to unpleasant and sometimes extreme developments, such as rioting on college campuses, it is basically a healthy and useful phenomenon for youth and for society. It is all too soon that the questing, inquisitive mind and the lively spirit become tamed and harnessed to everyday problems, never to soar again. Those of us who have passed this phase need the stimulus from the young to keep us from stagnating and indeed, to rejuvenate us through frequent confrontation.

As necessary and healthy as youthful forays onto new frontiers may be, the hazards are well known to older generations. At least some members of each generation must learn painfully from experience why society places certain limits on behavior. The ideological crusade sometimes turns into new forms of intolerance. The search for new experience may become no more than a quest for sensual

[1] Reprinted with permission from *Medical Times*, Vol. 97, No. 8.

pleasure. Many have observed that each generation discovers sex anew and regards it as its own original invention. The pleasures of freedom from restraint in this area, as in others, are far more quickly appreciated than are the long-term consequences of behavior and the need for responsibility as well as for freedom.

In escaping from the usual conventions, youth often become entrapped in new types of conformity. In abandoning traditional values, they may create and follow false prophets. During the past few years, we have been seeing a plague sweeping across the country in the form of widespread use of powerful and dangerous drugs. This is a major sociological problem with serious medical consequences. The drug movement has its own ideology, and of course, its own prophets, who offer their followers the prospects of expanded consciousness, religious revelation and delightful new dimensions to experience.

The high priest and pied piper of this movement is a former psychologist whose name is now known to everyone, Timothy Leary.

Here are a few of the statements made by Leary in a lengthy interview, published in *Playboy* magazine several years ago.[2]

Playboy: "A great deal of what is said about LSD by its proponents, including you, has been couched in terms of religious mysticism. You spoke earlier, in fact, of discovering 'divinity' through LSD. In what way is the LSD experience religious?"

Leary: "It depends on what you mean by religion. For almost everyone, the LSD experience is a confrontation with new forms of wisdom and energy that dwarf and humiliate man's mind. This experience of awe and revelation is often described as religious. I consider my work basically religious, because it has as its goal the systematic expansion of consciousness and the discovery of energies within, which men call 'divine.' From the psychedelic point of view almost all religions are attempts—sometimes limited temporally or nationally—to discover the inner potential. Well, LSD is Western yoga. The aim of all Eastern religion, like the aim of LSD, is basically to get high: that is, to expand your consciousness and find ecstasy and revelation within. . . .

---

[2] Excerpted from "Playboy Interview: Timothy Leary," *Playboy* Magazine (September 1966); copyright © 1966 by Playboy. Used by permission.

"An enormous amount of energy from every fiber of your body is released under LSD—most especially including sexual energy. There is no question that LSD is the most powerful aphrodisiac ever discovered by man. . . .

"When you're making love under LSD, it's as though every cell in your body—and you have trillions—is making love with every cell in her body. Your hand doesn't caress her skin but sinks down into and merges with ancient dynamos of ecstasy within her."

At another point in the interview:

Playboy: "We've heard that some women who ordinarily have difficulty achieving orgasm find themselves capable of multiple orgasms under LSD. Is that true?"
Leary: "In a carefully prepared, loving LSD session, a woman will inevitably have several hundred orgasms."
Playboy: "Several hundred?"
Leary: "Yes, several hundred."

With propaganda like that coming at them from all directions, is it any wonder that many of our youth have been unable to resist the temptation to take a cosmic hayride with LSD?

There are, of course, a tremendous number of drugs, some of which have been known since ancient times, which can affect man's mental state in various ways. Some of them have been incorporated into religious ceremonies by various peoples, and others, most notoriously, alcohol and opium, have been viewed both as blessings and curses upon mankind, by various peoples throughout history. One of the earliest recorded accounts of drug abuse, you may remember, is the biblical description of Noah's drunkenness after he and his family escaped from the flood.

A preliminary review of drugs reported to the Maryland Psychiatric Case Register for an eight-month period covers a list of seventy-seven drugs. This extensive list of drugs which have been misused includes synthetic and natural substances with a wide range of pharmacologic actions. Some have medicinal value when used legitimately and some do not. There is no single age group that is subject to drug abuse, but the types of drugs used, tend to vary according to age and other factors. There can be no doubt that we live in a drug-taking world. Drug use and abuse have long been widespread among nearly all age groups. What is new is the widespread use of "psychedelic" substances, especially among middle-class youth. While the abuse of other drugs may have serious consequences, new types of problems have been created by the "psychedelic" substances.

There are a number of drugs in use among the psychedelic generation. These include LSD, amphetamines, marijuana and many others which can be easily obtained on the blackmarket. Here is a partial list of such substances:

LSD-25	STP (DOM)
Marijuana	Morning glory seeds
Mescaline (Peyote)	Amphetamine
Psylocybin	Methedrine
Nutmeg	Cocaine
DMT	Belladonna

Although their pharmacological actions are complicated and variable, most of them have some stimulant effects, as opposed to say alcohol which is primarily a depressant. In a great many cases, the user takes an unknown dose of an unknown drug or mixture of drugs. All of these drugs are dangerous and can lead to serious psychiatric disturbances, despite contrary claims of such authorities as Allen Ginsberg, the hippie poet. Psychiatric complications, although not universal, are numerous and vary with the drug and the personality of the patient.

The full extent of drug use is unknown. Estimates range from 15 percent of college students upward to over 50 percent who experiment with them. A smaller number become regular users. The use is, of course, not limited to students, but tends to follow the middle class. The lower class seem to prefer the delights of heroin to those of LSD, although their use of marijuana and amphetamines, and other drugs, is by no means uncommon.

There are no really good statistics on the drug abuse problem. In preliminary studies from the Maryland Psychiatric Case Register about 4 percent of patients attending psychiatric facilities in Maryland have problems which include drug dependency of some sort. This figure is likely to be on the low side, since reporting of this information is inadequate and often neglected. Some psychiatric facilities in various localities report very high rates. The Psychiatric Emergency Service at the University of California, Los Angeles as of last year was running about 20 percent of its cases involving complications of such drugs as LSD.[3] Bellevue Hospital in New York also has reported large series of cases. The Department of Psychiatry at Temple University in Philadelphia also sees a fairly large number of cases, both as outpatients and inpatients. Approximately 15 percent of our psychiatric outpatients have recent histories of using such drugs as LSD, amphetamines, and marijuana. Marijuana is by far the most popular of these drugs. LSD use is less common, but by no means rare. These patients show a wide variety of psychiatric syndromes, which I will discuss in somewhat more detail later.

I would like to digress briefly to touch upon a few historical points without going into the long, involved and rather fascinating history of drug use in various cultures, or discussing the many drugs which have been used by various primitive and modern peoples. LSD in many ways is the most interesting of the drugs under discussion. It is certainly the most powerful in terms of the dose response curve, although there are a number of other drugs which produce rather similar effects. As you know LSD was synthesized in Switzerland in 1938 and is an ergot derivative. The history books tell of mass epidemics of insanity occurring in Europe during the Middle Ages. These epidemics were due to ergotism caused by mouldy wheat, and were also accompanied by a variety of somatic manifestations. Another epidemic occurred in a small town in France not too many years ago.

When the psychological effects of LSD were accidentally discovered in the 1940's, further experiments were carried out on humans and it was thought that a drug had been found which could produce schizophrenia in normal people. This view was later modified, but it contributed to the search for drugs which could be used in the treatment of psychiatric illnesses, such as schizophrenia. Chlorpromazine was discovered independently but it is of some interest that this drug is useful both for treating the symptoms of LSD intoxication and for schizophrenia.

Somewhat later the United States Army became seriously interested in LSD as a chemical warfare agent. So powerful was this drug that they reasoned it could be used to disable enemy troops and pop-

---

[3] Told to me by Dr. Duke Fisher of UCLA.

ulations without firing a shot and without killing them. Meanwhile, some psychiatrists and other people interested in mental illness began studying the use of LSD as an adjunct to treating psychiatric patients. It seems somewhat of a paradox that a drug which was demonstrated to cause mental disturbance was considered by some as an aid in curing it. The status of LSD as an adjunct to the treatment of certain mental disorders is still under study and considerably more information is needed before very much can be said about its usefulness. In any case, it has not gained wide acceptance. LSD has been useful, however, as a tool for studying psychological functions and also as an aid in unraveling the biochemistry and neurophysiology of the brain. I have been interested in this subject since the mid-1950's when I became engaged in basic science studies with LSD and related drugs with a group at the University of Maryland Department of Psychiatry. At that time we could never have imagined what the next decade was to bring.

It is a profound irony that a drug which has been shown to cause severe mental derangement and which was considered a strong candidate as a chemical warfare agent in the 1950's, has been hailed as the source of expanded consciousness, wisdom and delight for mankind in the 1960's. The irony is particularly poignant for those of us who repeatedly see the tragic consequences of this large-scale misadventure.

I mentioned earlier that the psychiatric complications associated with abuse of these drugs are quite variable and are associated with the drug and with the personality of the person using it. The circumstances in which he takes the drug, of course, also have an influence. Individuals of unstable personality are most likely to develop serious complications. These drugs do not always produce lasting psychiatric complications *de novo*. More often they bring out latent problems or heighten existing ones. Borderline schizophrenics who may function in a fairly adequate manner may develop full blown psychoses after taking one of them. Sociopaths may become even more antisocial, and so forth. Some individuals who are slipping into mental illness may use these drugs in misguided efforts to help themselves, and of course only compound their difficulties. Individuals of sounder make-up are likely to develop more subtle disturbances from drug use. It is seldom possible to make a clear distinction between the long-term drug effects and the part played by the patient's pre-existing personality difficulties.

The complications of LSD use include:

1. *Acute psychotic and panic states* while the subject is under the influence of the drug. Such reactions are sometimes, but not often, accompanied by suicidal, homicidal, or other antisocial behavior.
2. *Prolonged psychotic reactions* following drug use. Often requiring hospitalization.
3. *Brief recurrences of the LSD reaction* for weeks to months following drug use. This may include hallucinatory experiences, difficulties in concentration, and changes in mood.
4. *The dropout syndrome,* which consists of prolonged states of poor concentration, apathy, loss of goals and indolence.
5. *Brain damage* has not been conclusively demonstrated to result from LSD use, but investigators suspect that subtle chemical lesions of the brain may be responsible for some of the prolonged behavioral disturbances.
6. *Chromosomal damage.* This is a subject of considerable interest. The evidence for it is not conclusive but there is the possibility that LSD use may cause such effects, which pose a risk for the user and for his offspring.

The effects of marijuana are milder than those of LSD, but similar in quality and the complications are also similar though they tend to be less common and less severe. Perhaps the commonest effect is the "dropout syndrome" which is a combined effect of drug use and the social milieu of many users, which encourages dropping out of society. Marijuana can, at times, precipitate psychotic reactions. One reason why marijuana does not give more difficulty is that most of the marijuana available in this country is of a low grade and may have little more than a placebo effect in many instances. The term hashish is applied to the resin derived from the flowering tops of the cannabis, but extracts of other portions of the plant apparently may also be sold as "hash." Hashish is considerably more potent than leaves since it contains a higher concentration of tetrahydrocannabinol, the active ingredient.

The argument is often rasied that marijuana use, while occasionally leading to complications, is less harmful than alcohol and therefore should be legalized, and even encouraged. Alcoholism is, of course, a problem of major dimensions in our society, so this argument may at first glance seem convincing. Further examination shows it to be fallacious. Marijuana is certainly far from harmless, as much clinical and experimental evidence attests. In any case, there is no reason to assume that it is an antidote to alcoholism. We already have a great enough problem with alcohol. What do we need with an additional problem?

Marijuana use does not inevitably lead to crime or to narcotics, as its apologists like to point out in debunking a widespread myth. It does, however, often lead to the use of other dangerous stimulants and hallucinogenic drugs, and in some cases to narcotics. When this happens it is a result, not of marijuana use, per se, but of complex psychological and social factors surrounding the use of mari juana.

The amphetamines are widely abused and lead to serious complications especially when taken in large doses over extended periods of time. Jitteriness and sleeplessness occur unless counteracted by depressant drugs such as barbiturates, which add further complications. Psychotic reactions involving hallucinations and delusions occur commonly in amphetamine users. In many instances these reactions cannot be easily distinguished from spontaneously occurring schizophrenic psychoses.

Amphetamines, marijuana and the hallucinogenic drugs are not physiologically addicting and there are no withdrawal symptoms in the usual sense when use is terminated. There is no specific form of treatment for complications resulting from use of these drugs. In each case, the treatment has to be designed according to the particular symptoms demonstrated by the patient. If there is agitation, for example, sedation or tranquilization may be necessary. Psychotic reactions are dealt with the usual ways, and so forth. Long-term management is often extremely difficult with these patients, because a large proportion of them return to their old friends and habits and continue to use drugs. It is still too early to say what the long-term prognosis will be for this group of patients.

Many physicians have been, or will be, consulted by anguished parents about their youngsters who may have been using drugs. Very often the parents are overwhelmed with feelings of guilt, and a sense of failure. They want to know, "Where did we go wrong?" I have seen "acidheads" and "pot smokers" from every sort of family background. They come from families that are strict and families that are permissive; religious and non-religious; intact and broken; homes filled with love and homes filled with hate. Perhaps this is a sign of the weakening of family influence. In any case, the parents are not entitled to all the blame. This is an angry generation, and one way they have for expressing anger is through self-destructive behavior, which shatters all their parents' visions and hopes for them. While parents may be unable to adopt an attitude of unconcern, they should be warned that their own self-flagellation is not only useless but may be part of the payoff their children get from deviant behavior.

For this problem as for other medical problems, the best treatment is prevention. Unfortunately we don't know much about how to prevent it from developing and spreading. Some people believe that it is already on the wane. This may be true in a few areas, but I don't know of any evidence that the extent of the problem is diminishing in general. I can assure you we are still seeing plenty of it in Philadelphia. (I should add, that as serious as the drug problem may be, there is no need to fear that the current generation of youth is a lost one. Most of our young people, including many who flirt with drugs without getting hooked, are solid, healthy citizens.) Control of drug traffic by law enforcement agencies has not been generally effective, and for some young people it even serves as an inducement since there is nothing they like better than a sense of adventure and the opportunity to flirt with danger. There is some hope that education of young people with respect to the hazards of drug abuse may be of some value, and some films and other materials have been developed for this purpose. Unfortunately, we are contending with powerful educational forces working in the opposite direction. In general, these other sources of misinformation and propaganda are more likely to carry weight with some young people who distrust everything that comes from responsible members of what they call the "Establishment."

One small hopeful sign is the development of student organizations to distribute responsible and accurate information on drugs with advice from authorities in the field. Hopefully this will prove to be of some value. I think our greatest hope lies in the inconstancy of youth. As a new crop of young people come along, the drug scene with all the publicity it has had for some years now, should begin to look rather out of date and foolish to them. They will be looking for new frontiers and new adventures. While it will not disappear entirely, I predict that the drug scene will, in time, gradually dwindle in magnitude. This should not be taken as an invitation to complacency, however, since today's drug problem may be replaced tomorrow by others, at least equally alarming. By then most of today's youth will have settled into responsible positions. They will shake their heads with alarm and sorrow just as we do, and wonder, "Where in heaven's name is the world heading?"

CHAPTER 2

IS THAT A CREATURE IN THERE?

IS THAT A CREATURE IN THERE?
BY T. GUTHRIE SPEERS, JR., B.D.

I was never prouder of the leaders of the church I serve in New Canaan than I was early last fall when the elders and deacons of our church met to consider the request of a group called "Genesis" to use rooms in our building for their program aimed at helping teenagers threatened by drugs, aimed really to let those teenagers help themselves through various group encounters, under professional supervision. In that meeting of our officers, we began by talking about *them,* about those kids who have been on drugs and are trying to kick the habit, about those kids particularly tempted by drugs (and there are mighty few today not tempted), and about the problems that could arise and certainly had to be faced if these kids were to be meeting regularly in our building. But then the direction of our discussion began to change. We stopped talking so much about *them,* and began talking more about *us,* admitting freely to each other that our own kids are threatened by drugs, that some from our own families have been caught in the horrid clutches of some of these drugs, that we know something in ourselves of what this confusion and emptiness and longing in these kids is like, and that therefore we want them in our building, where perhaps something of their longing, basically for love, can be met. Finally we came to a vote, and all those elders and deacons, including those who had had very real questions about this and had very rightly expressed those questions, all joined together, unanimously, to invite "Genesis" to make their home with us.

I was so proud that night not just because we had invited "Genesis," but also because we, the officers of that church, had seen *their* problem as *our* problem, their hangups at least similar to our own hangups, their confusion and emptiness and longing not unlike our own confusion and emptiness and longing. For once we began to recognize our own kids in these troubled kids, we began to recognize ourselves as well: all of us in our own way looking for some sense of meaning and purpose, for some sense of the worthwhileness of life itself in a world that increasingly treats human life as cheap and shallow and expendable. When that realization comes home to us who are adults, we at least are open—and will make our churches open—to those of the younger generation caught up in drugs as we have been caught up in alcohol, or in sleeping pills, or in the ever so false and feeble attempts to prove ourselves so very successful.

I am no expert on the drug scene. I don't feel I've gotten anywhere with many of those young people in our church who have become seriously involved with drugs. But I have tried to keep open to them, while encouraging them and their parents to seek professional help. And I've tried to keep at least some lines open between them and their parents, and some sense of perspective toward some laws cruelly and ridiculously harsh, in terms of drug use. This surely is the job of all of us who try to be ministers of reconciliation. And most of all, I've sought to help parents and teenagers, long before any crisis comes with regard to drugs, to learn to know and love each other, to respect and trust each other, to enjoy each other and each other's different ways. For it is out of such relationships, across the generations, that we have a chance, as churchmen, to keep those of both generations from becoming addicted to drugs or to any other form of escape from this exciting business of being alive.

Last winter, my wife and I and our three sons and daughter, ranging in age from fourteen down to eight, spent a glorious day cross-country skiing in the Adirondacks. We skied the whole length of the Lower Ausable Lake, which we have often rowed down in the summer, and near the far end came to a lean-to, where in summer we've often stopped for a picnic and a swim. That lean-to had the most enormous drift of snow across its front. But our twelve-year-old son, Tom, who was in the lead, managed to crawl inside one corner of the lean-to. Then when our ten-year-old, Sam, came along, Tom hollered to him from out of those depths, in an eerie ghostlike voice. Sam, more than ready to play the game, called back, "Is that a creature in there?" "Yes," was the reply. "And what kind of a creature?" Sam asked. In that second or two before Tom answered, I thought of what I might have said in those circumstances: "a fierce wild beast," or "the abominable snowman." But Tom's answer was far better, and came out loud and clear. What kind of a creature was he? "A person," he said. What more are we here to do than to convince parents and children alike to know and accept and love each other as persons, each one known and accepted and loved by God himself? And how better to try to cope with this whole growing and frightening problem of drug abuse?

Some weeks ago, one evening after supper, I sat down with two of my sons to listen straight through all four sides of the recording of "Jesus Christ: Superstar." I don't want to say much about that recording now except that I was singularly impressed by it, and since then, we have played it in our church itself, with the volume up high and with the words in our hands, which was quite a time for all of us, young and old alike. But over and beyond the exciting and sometimes moving experience of listening right through this rock opera that first evening, was the experience of listening to it with those two sons of mine, all three of us following the words intently. We hadn't set out to do this together. We hadn't planned this as a family event. Actually, only half the family was involved, and that half quite by chance. Yet, once the three of us were settled in that couch and utterly wound up together in "Superstar," nothing was going to get us up and away until those four sides of the recording were finished.

And I mean quite literally nothing. Not even the telephone. Not even elders of the church calling up on important church business. Some did call that evening. But when they did, and some member of the non-listening half of our family came running in to tell me, I simply said to say I was busy and would call back later. That made an impression on both halves of the family, on the listeners and non-listeners alike. Not to go to the phone, that tyrant we so seldom dare to ignore, and not to go to the phone when an elder was calling, and not to go because those two kids on either side there on the couch, and being wound up with them in that music, were more important—that made a rather astounding impression. And the reason it did is that all kinds of other people, all kinds of other activities, sometimes just plain being tired, get in the way of our really paying attention to our children, and to our wives or husbands, and to other people *as people,* and thus get in the way of our demonstrating how deeply we do care about them, how deeply we do give a damn about them.

Arnold Come of San Francisco Seminary said recently:

I am suggesting to you that the most critical, the central mission of the Church in the 1970's is simply this: to be the community that gives a damn. . . . The most frightening reality that I encounter as I go about the land and about the world, is really not the population explosion, or the threat of starvation, or the endless wars, or the generation gap, or space travel. What frightens me is this pervasive mood of despair, of everybody withdrawing into their own private life and giving that good phrase "Do your own thing" that wrong twist which means "I don't give a damn about anybody else." [1]

All through his ministry, right on to the cross itself, Jesus made it abundantly clear that he did give a damn about all sorts and kinds of people. A case in point is Levi and his fellow tax collectors, basically a bunch of small-time crooks. What they saw in Jesus, most amazingly and almost unbelievably, was someone who did notice and was concerned for and gave a damn about the likes of them. When you know full well that most everyone else hates your guts, and couldn't care less, and doesn't give a damn about you, it makes all the difference in the world to have Jesus give a damn. That's precisely the difference Jesus did make in the lives of those tax collectors.

You remember how Luke tells this story. "After this he went out, and saw a tax collector named Levi, sitting at the tax office." Do you catch what this is saying, the amazing thing this is saying? Jesus *saw* that tax collector. He noticed. He cared. He gave a damn. Levi was just sitting there, at a little table, reaching out for all he could get, naturally hated and even more naturally avoided if at all possible by those going by who didn't want him to get his filthy clutches on them. Jesus saw him, and walked straight up to him, and looked into his eyes with a look Levi had never seen before, and spoke with a love Levi had never felt before, and said: "Come on, Levi. I need you as one of my disciples." And Levi, who had never been told by anyone

---

[1] Arnold Come, *Thesis Theological Cassette* Vol. 1, No. 10. Used by permission.

before that he was needed, got up from that crummy little table a new man, a real man, a real human being—and all because Jesus had given a damn about him.

Now look what happens next. Jesus has a new disciple. But immediately that disciple makes demands upon him. You can't expect to give a damn one moment and then the next to go your own way again, not as a pastor, not as a parent. There's more to giving a damn than that. In this case, that more was getting involved in a fantastic dinner party at Levi's house, to which he had invited lots of other creepy characters—tax collectors—like himself. What other plans Jesus had for that evening we do not know. But he threw them all aside. He threw everything aside. And he gave himself to that party, giving a damn for every person there, letting every person there know how much he mattered as a person, mattered at that moment when Jesus was talking with him more than any other person, mattered finally as a person to God himself. Jesus brought salvation to that motley crew, not by castigating them for their sins—they knew what slobs they were; everyone was forever telling them that—but by stopping to notice them, by stopping to give them his wholehearted and enthusiastic and appreciative attention, by stopping to listen and to love and to laugh together, to give a damn.

I would suggest that in many of our communities, where there are probably too many elaborate carefully planned parties, we haven't nearly enough spur-of-the-moment spontaneous parties, just the sort in which Jesus threw everything else aside to enjoy the time with Levi and his friends that evening. We need to have some such parties with our own children, stopping everything else, even that pest of a telephone, to turn a simple supper or perhaps the listening to records of an evening into a family celebration, where we won't have to say—because it will be perfectly obvious—that we do give a damn for one another. Other such parties—equally spontaneous and yet perhaps requiring an occasional meeting to be skipped and an occasional sneaking away early from the office and even an occasional ignoring of a somewhat messy house and not worrying about whether that house is a suitable spot for a party—we need to have, again with our children, particularly the teenagers among them, but also with a few friends of various ages thrown in as well, from other teenagers right on up the age scale, because our little families are too little and often too brittle to survive by themselves. If it was a motley crew at Levi's house that evening, it could be just as marvelously motley a crew at our houses most any evening, sitting around a big bowl of spaghetti, across differences in age and outlook, fascinated with those differences in age and outlook, talking to each other, listening to each other, getting a kick out of each other, giving a damn for each other. This is the only sort of approach I know in trying to deal with the drug problem before it becomes a problem, before there is that unbearable confusion and emptiness and longing that lead people to drugs.

Once a month those of us in our town especially concerned with young people—school administrators and teachers, pastors, community leaders—meet for a morning of discussion. Last month we met with a group of articulate and appealing high-school students. The charge was made by some of them and by some of us, that all too many parents in our town don't give a damn about their children. There were those who sought to refute that charge by pointing to the many marvelous facilities, including the fine new YMCA building in which we were meeting, that parents have provided for their children, at a considerable sacrifice of money and effort. But that seemed to me to miss the point, and it was then that I began thinking of that evening a few nights before when I had put everything and every one else aside to listen to "Superstar" with two of my sons. It was the unusualness of that evening that hit me. How few other such evenings, how few other such occasions I could point to over the past few months when my children had had my undivided attention, when I had made it perfectly obvious to them by my interest in them and by my appreciation of them *as real persons* that I did give a damn about them. Looking back, I had to admit to myself that not in any intentional way and certainly not in any malicious way, but simply by not stopping to notice and to pay attention and to care, I really hadn't been giving much of a damn about my kids. That hurt, as it should hurt. All I can say is we certainly had one great family supper in our house that night, and I am thankful, for his sake or hers, that no poor soul tried to telephone in the midst of it.

Then a couple of weeks ago, in the home of one of our church families, we gathered together one evening a lively mixture of people: four high-school students, one college student, one young couple in their early twenties, six of us obviously middle-aged parents, and one spirited still-jogging grandmother in her eighties. We simply talked, over a wide range of subjects. There were strangers to all of us in that group. But before the evening ended, a measure of trust had been established, so that that college student who had been picked up by the police (I would say in a rather sneaky and uncalled for way) a year ago and had been brought to trial simply for having a hashish pipe in his car admitted to having been arrested, and further admitted that he felt no remorse for what he had done, except for the pain he had caused his parents. Then I admitted to feeling no remorse for having broken the law by speeding to get to that gathering that night. And we were off, all of us, on a heated discussion of the validity of certain laws, on whether and when and how they should be broken. We were far from agreeing when we finally broke up, but that didn't matter. What mattered was that we had dared to be honest with each other, and that we had tried to listen to and to learn from each other, respecting each other as persons, regardless of age. It was a wonderful experience, and a renewing and reviving experience for everyone there. It didn't solve any of our hangups. But we honestly shared some of them. And that surely is a step toward their solution, in that sort of larger family group (a good definition of the church) and in our individual families too.

Our families have a way of catching up with us. Our children have a way of catching up with us, and if we are not careful and have not learned to know them as persons, they may leave us behind, perhaps to enter that strange and alien world of drugs. Robert Capon, that delightful Anglican priest-writer of theological cookbooks, describes the process:

> The portrait of a young couple with their first baby is still an elegant one. But the snapshot of a pair of beaten forty-five-year-olds surrounded, overshadowed, and stymied by a handful of teenagers and a clutch of elementary-school pupils had less to recommend it on the level of intelligibility. Somewhere in between, elegance left by the back door. Around the end of toddling and the beginning of talking, a second and unnoticed pregnancy began; another and quite painless delivery was accomplished. A *person* was born. A piece of history began to distinguish itself and quietly proceeded to start a history of its own.[2]

These are busy hectic days for all of us, and confusing days and tiring days and often discouraging days as well. But Jesus' days were

[2] From *An Offering of Uncles* by Robert F. Capon, © Sheed and Ward Inc., 1967. Used by permission.

all those things too. And yet he always found time, he always made time, he always took time, to treat people as persons, to take them seriously, to listen to them and appreciate them, to give a damn about them—and this regardless of who they were, their age, their background, their position or lack of it in society. Jesus would have us do likewise, beginning in our own families and with our own children, entering into their histories and letting them enter into ours, and then going out as families to include friends of different ages and out of different situations, to make them part of our larger family, a larger family like the smaller family, where people are persons before they are adults or children, or anything else, and are respected and loved as such, where all of us do take the time and make the effort to give a damn about each other. This won't solve the drug problem. But it will make us all much more sensitive to that problem, and to each other in the process.

CHAPTER 3

ATTITUDES, DRUGS,
AND DRUG ABUSE

CHAPTER 3

ATTITUDES, DRUGS, AND DRUG ABUSE

BY HENRY S. G. CUTTER, PH.D.

The behavioral effects of drugs cannot be explained solely on a physiological or chemical level. These effects are more readily interpretable when one takes into account the attitudes, expectations, and values surrounding drug-taking. From this perspective it may become clearer to the reader that the physiological addiction to drugs is only part of the drug problem, and consequently detoxification is only part of the solution to it.

Patterns of drug use and attitudes toward drug use are culturally conditioned and are dependent on factors such as group membership, social and individual values, personality, and the expectations surrounding the effects of drugs.

Attitude is a particularly appropriate concept for analyzing drug use and drug effects because it spans and integrates the psychological and physiological aspects of the problem. The concept "attitude" is a useful shorthand way of referring to a complex of social and personal processes. The definition of attitude outlines many of the useful ideas necessary for understanding human drug-taking.

An attitude is usually defined as a state of readiness, a tendency to act or react in a certain manner when appropriately stimulated.[1] Attitudes are always present but are dormant much of the time, and are aroused only in the presence of a relevant subject. Reading a book on drug abuse, or contacting someone whom one suspects is using drugs are examples of actions which are sufficient to arouse one's various attitudes toward drugs. It may be said that attitudes have

---

[1] A. N. Oppenheim, *Questionnaire Design and Attitude Measurement* (New York: Basic Books, 1966).

three facets or components: (1) attitudes have a *cognitive component* (belief, expectation, or set); they also have (2) an *emotional component* (strong feelings or mood); and (3) an *action component* (various forms of behavior).

Attitudes vary in strength, a fact that is clearly recognized when attitude change is attempted through communication, advertising, education, psychotherapy, group process, alcohol, and drugs. More extreme attitudes, both positive and negative, tend to be held with greater vehemence. Attitudes vary in their endurance and in their stability—they are stable in some areas and unstable in others.

Attitudes vary in depth from the more superficial level of belief, to the deeper level of values, down to the hidden recesses of personality. Attitudes are rarely logical or well thought out; they reflect strong feelings or what might be called "psychologic." Compatible with their social and cultural origins, attitudes are usually acquired or modified by acting on or reacting to other people, either singly or in groups.

As with attitudes, drugs also have their principal impact through the manipulation of feelings and mood. Their physiological effects to some extent mimic the consequences of various naturally occurring pleasurable activities such as eating or sex. Natural or drug-induced feelings of satisfaction can be conditioned in a variety of ways to lead to a variety of experiences. When drugs bring feelings of satisfaction, they may be sought to supplement or replace other satisfactions. It should also be noted that dissatisfaction, resulting from frustration, can also be modified by a variety of activities including drugs.

Drugs can be divided, roughly speaking, into three types: (1) stimulants that serve to increase the activity of the nervous system, (2) depressants that decrease nervous-system activity, and (3) the psychedelics that distort nervous-system activity.

It is at this point that we must integrate the independent discussions of attitudes and drugs if we are to understand the effects of drugs on human behavior. Fortunately there are a variety of experimental studies that clarify the interaction between drug effects and attitudes.

These studies all have their origins in the study of placebos—inert substances that are usually made to look like pills—that can have a powerful effect on patients.

For centuries, people in the healing professions, both modern physicians and primitive witch doctors, have known that treatments, even ineffective treatments, given with proper ritual and confidence, can bring relief particularly to problems of psychogenic origin. The placebo effect seems to be based on the patient's favorable expectations as to the effects of the drug originating from the communications of the physician or prior belief system. Perhaps this is why even modern medicine depends on a good "bedside manner."

Double blind studies, where neither the investigator nor the subject knows if the drug in question has actually been administered or if a placebo was given instead, are a research necessity, following the discovery that the experimenter's expectations and knowledge of treatment condition can subtly (and sometimes not so subtly) bias the results of a drug study.

Schacter and Singer[2] in their work on the cognitive labeling of the drug effects, find that the type of drug (whether a stimulant or a depressant) is irrelevant to the effect which the subject experiences. In other words, the experimental instructions that the drug being administered is calming or arousing (independent of its stimulant or depressant nature) determine the subject's experience of the drug.

Cutter and Kola[3] in a double blind study involving alcohol find that there is a very complex interaction of personality variables (e.g., sociability and impulsivity) with expectations of the subjects as to the effects of alcohol, as well as with the physiological effects of alcohol in their joint effect on risk-taking behavior.

The setting in which one takes drugs is extremely important to the kinds of experiences one has. Thus, LSD taken in cold, clinical settings may lead to bad "trips," while pleasant, acceptant atmospheres seem to lead to good "trips." Our experimental subjects tell us that drinking beverage alcohol in a laboratory setting is a very different experience from drinking in a bar: having two ounces of bourbon in a well-lit, somewhat sterile research office is less glamorous and attractive than drinking in a dimly lit neighborhood "hangout."

This brief report of the research literature and our own laboratory experience clearly indicates that attitudes toward drugs, doctors, and

[2] S. Schacter and J. Singer, "Cognitive, Social and Physiological Determinants of Emotional State," *Psychological Review,* Vol. 69 (1962), pp. 379–97.
[3] H. S. G. Cutter and L. Kola, "Alcohol, Drinking Set, Personality and Risk" (unpublished manuscript, 1971).

drug experimenters are implicated in understanding drug effects. Attitudes are even more strongly implicated in coping with the problems associated with drug use. As noted earlier, attitudes are established or modified by interaction among people. Attitudes are shaped directly through face-to-face contact or indirectly through some other form of communication.

There is no doubt that attitudes shape actions. A policeman, for example, who views drug addicts (junkies) as less than human is more likely to use his nightstick when arresting an addict than a policeman with more benevolent attitudes. Battered addicts in turn, receive an indelibly negative attitude modification toward police and other authorities. The problem gets even more subtle and convoluted when one realizes that addicts may have hostile attitudes toward the police—acquired from their peer group—that antedate any contact with the police. This hostility may actually stimulate punishment by the police, who otherwise might have conducted an arrest in a routine and professional manner. This phenomenon, where expectations lead to the events expected, has been labeled the "self-fulfilling prophecy."

Self-fulfilling prophecies can also be observed among parents who, finding their children have experimented with drugs, indicate to them that they are worthless bums. The children respond with the "psychologic" syllogism, "I am worthless, worthless people use drugs, therefore I use drugs." In this manner, parents—although unintentionally—often increase the vulnerability of their children to drug dependence.

Another way in which parents seem to foster drug use by their children is by giving their children attitudinal "double messages" about drugs: the parents' frequent warnings about the hazards of drugs may only serve to make drugs more psychologically salient and attractive.

Drug use in our society is an emotional issue loaded with conflicts and contradictions of long standing. Prohibition, the legalization of marijuana, and the control of heroin are issues that reflect the ambivalence in our country toward the use of our legal system in controlling personal behavior. Although breaking the law is repugnant to most Americans, the use of one's drug of choice is viewed as an inalienable right. The multiple approaches to the drug problem—viewing it alternately as a medical problem, a moral defect, a problem of

building sufficient jail cells to contain all the pushers and users—
suggest a major failure to sort out feelings and thoughts toward drug
use among members of all social classes.

No effective social action toward solving the drug problem can be
taken until people explore with each other their relevant thoughts
and feelings, evaluate them, and arrive at a consensus as to a plan of
action that can be carried out. Until this process occurs among
sufficiently large segments of society, police efforts to "dry up" the
drug trade are going to be impeded by a natural reluctance to turn in
friends or relatives who are breaking the law. Community members
are going to continue their vehement opposition to self-help efforts
by addicts and ex-addicts in establishing treatment facilities unless
the community members themselves are actively involved. Teachers
concerned about drug use among their students will still have to walk
a tight-rope between the school administration, the police, and the
parents. Clergymen will continue to encounter considerable flak from
parishioners when they attempt to set up teenage "drop in" centers
in their churches and synagogues. Medically administered methadone programs will continue to be viewed by some members of the
black community merely as a new method of enslavement.

Our experience with leaderless discussion groups consisting of
five to eight clergymen and educators in each group suggests that
sharing and comparing one's own attitudes toward drugs with others
is not an easy task and that coming to a consensus on a course of
action that they could follow in their respective work situations was
an impossible task in the time allotted. Although the group members
had been explicitly instructed to explore their own attitudes toward
drugs, there was a general tendency to turn toward a visible "expert"
(usually a doctor or a nurse) for answers. The expertise of the "authorities" was rapidly exhausted and the groups' attitudes were observed to split between those favoring fundamentalist or legalist as
opposed to sociological or psychological explanations of the drug
problem.

It is most interesting to note that discussion of one's own drinking
habits and drug use apparently was too difficult for the group participants to face up to and consequently was avoided.

When the small groups were convened into one larger group to
discuss the plans for action that the subgroups were supposed to
have evolved, it readily became apparent that this had been an im-

possible task. By the end of the session, the experience by the clergy and educators of their own conflicting attitudes led them to appreciate the difficulties in exploring the drug problem and the need for the personal and social clarification of attitudes toward drugs.

CHAPTER 4

DRUGS, RATIONALITY, AND THE LAW

DRUGS, RATIONALITY, AND THE LAW
BY GORDON A. MARTIN, JR., J.D.

I should like to focus my remarks on the administration of justice and the law-enforcement aspects of the drug problem and particularly upon the setting of priorities within these areas. Just how are we exercising these priorities? Consider how New York City's 1970–71 criminal justice budget is being spent: 51.2 percent of the funds are spent on police patrol, 12.3 percent on crime investigation, 6.6 percent on traffic law enforcement, 6.6 percent on confinement, and 4.1 percent on support. It is only after these needs have been met that we get to drug addiction treatment in a city that is reliably estimated to have over 100,000, and some believe more than 150,000, heroin addicts. A mere 3.7 percent of this budget is going into the area of drug addiction treatment; and way, way down on the list—the last significant item—one third of 1 percent is being spent for rehabilitation programs. We have had, for example, the benefit of the truly significant work that has been done by Dr. Vincent Dole and his wife, Dr. Marie Nyswander, both of Rockefeller University. These gifted people were principally responsible for the development of the methadone-blocking approach to heroin addiction, certainly the most significant step forward taken in drug treatment in the past decade. New York City also has produced such worthwhile psychotherapeutic residential programs as Daytop Village and Odyssey House. These organizations and certain similar ones have appeared to be delivering useful service, but not even they have been totally sure. Now for the first time in its history, the Association of Voluntary Agencies on Narcotics Treatment in New York City is planning a self-study so that we will be able to know precisely what these agencies are accomplishing.

One of the great problems in setting up treatment resources and funding programs for drug addiction is that once there is recognition that something is wrong and something has to be done, there is a tendency to spend money so quickly that all too often we don't take stock of how it is being spent and whether or not it is being spent on programs that work. In the process we neglect to establish an evaluation mechanism. This is a horrendous mistake, because if we do not seek independent evaluation of what we are doing, it is not unlikely that the funding source is going to dry up. If the crisis atmosphere and panic subside, governors, legislators, foundations, and the public may tire of expending their monies. Evaluation will also protect the successful program from the very real dual dangers of either exploitation or attack during political campaigns.

This self-study of these treatment agencies that has been announced will cost about $120,000. All of us can think of important ways in which that amount of money could be spent on the delivery of services. Yet I think there is no greater service that can be rendered than to determine just how effective the members of the Association of Voluntary Agencies on Narcotics Treatment really are. The director of one of these agencies—James Allen of Addicts Rehabilitation Center—has said, "If this thing shows I do not know what I am doing, then I'll get into a more gratifying field." All of us who work in this drug area must know, insofar as we can, what we are doing.

That is one set of priorities. We saw another set of priorities in the fall of 1969 when, for twenty-one days, the attorney general of the United States placed a disproportionately large number of agents from the Bureau of Narcotics and Dangerous Drugs on the Mexican border. The glorious name for that expedition was Operation Intercept, but it accomplished nothing except ill will on the part of tourists trying to cross the border and increased tension between the governments of the United States and of Mexico. When evaluating priorities in that situation, we should consider whether the Mexican border was the place where those agents could have been most useful or whether we would have preferred to have seen them assigned to one or more of our large cities on a crash basis. If, for example, these same agents had been placed under the control of Dick Callahan, the very able New England regional director of that agency, I think we could have completely eliminated heroin from the streets of the city of Boston for at least that period of time. But the emphasis was not on heroin. The emphasis was on marijuana. A priority had been set. But in my opinion, it was a sorely misplaced priority.

In sharp contrast, consider the priorities set by the Boston Police Department as demonstrated by the department's arrests in the city for 1969 and 1970. Chart A[1] includes all arrests for violations of the narcotics or marijuana laws, the line on top indicating narcotic arrests, the lower line marijuana arrests. In Boston, the right kind of priority had been set by law enforcement. Clearly the emphasis was on the violator of the narcotics laws. Chart B shows the arrests for the sale of heroin on the top line as opposed to the bottom line, arrests for the sale of marijuana. Again, it seems to me that the right priorities are being assigned. Finally, Chart C shows persons arrested for possession. The line at the top shows persons arrested for the illegal possession of heroin or opium or cocaine, whereas the line at the bottom indicates illegal possession of marijuana. These figures demonstrate how the members of Boston's vice and narcotics squad, as well as officers in the various precincts of the police department, were reacting to the sharp rise in the use of illegal drugs in that city during the same period in which federal authorities were still engaged in the folly of a last gasp drive against marijuana offenders. At least in the fall of 1969 the priorities of the Boston Police Department were substantially different from those of the federal authorities, and they were to remain so, though in greatly diminished degree, until the shocking reports of high levels of addiction among our servicemen in Vietnam made an overall federal reappraisal unavoidable.

What is the relationship of law enforcement to the courts with respect to the treatment of drug offenders? Allow me to describe to you a model probation officer working solely with addicted persons. Jerry Tordiglione of the East Boston District Court carries a case load of about eighty-five addicts. He exhibits a dedication to his charges and his community that is inspiring. He knows his probationers and their families. He knows the laws he must work under and the facilities and assistance available to him. He can judge which probationer needs which type of help. And he knows which of his charges shows signs

---

[1] Charts A, B, and C were prepared by Cheryl Dinneen, research assistant to the Coordinating Council on Drug Abuse, Boston, Massachusetts. Used by permission. (See pages 50–52.)

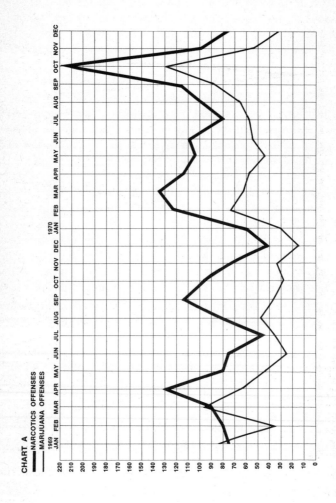

CHART A

NARCOTICS OFFENSES
MARIJUANA OFFENSES

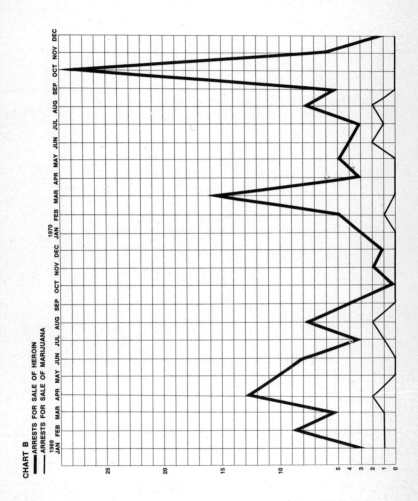

CHART B
ARRESTS FOR SALE OF HEROIN
ARRESTS FOR SALE OF MARIJUANA

CHART C

ARRESTS FOR ILLEGAL POSSESSION OF HEROIN, OPIUM, COCAINE, ETC.
ARRESTS FOR UNLAWFUL POSSESSION OF MARIJUANA

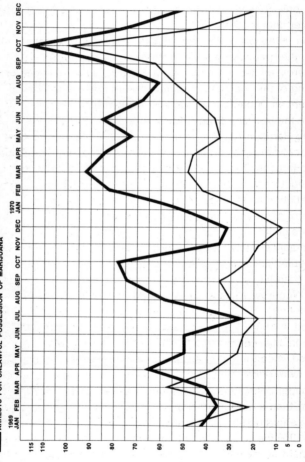

of returning to his drug habit. But obviously one individual, even with cooperative colleagues, is not able to handle all the drug problems of criminal offenders in even one section of a city. Almost one hundred years ago Massachusetts enacted the first statute anywhere in this country setting up a probation service in Boston with remarkably similar duties to what we might expect of probation officers today. However, only recently did the probation officer and drug offender encounter one another.

The invention of the hypodermic needle by Alexander Wood in 1843, the great excesses in narcotics use during the Civil War, and the heroin epidemic which followed at the end of that century and beginning of the twentieth century, all were major steps toward the enactment on December 17, 1914, of the first federal drug control legislation, the Harrison Drug Control Act.

The Harrison Act was intended to police the production and sale of narcotic drugs in order to limit their use for professional and scientific purposes. There was no provision for the treatment of addicts, and doctors and clinics engaging in such treatment encountered prosecution and harassment in the years that followed.

Throughout most of this century we have subscribed to the belief that we could tax drug habits out of existence. We saw this approach first manifest itself on the federal level with the Harrison Act, which was quite similar to legislation enacted in New York State in 1904. Less than five years after the Harrison Act—over the veto of President Woodrow Wilson—the Volstead Act made prohibition the law in this country. It was not a notable success and was, of course, repealed in 1933. The use of marijuana, however, remained perfectly legal in this country until 1937, when the marijuana tax act was passed. Alcohol had been given back to the people, but we had to take away something else. The marijuana tax act ultimately came a cropper constitutionally in *Leary* v *United States,* 395 US 6 (1969), but by then a hard-line penal approach to the drug offender had become engrained in the country.

In 1956 the Commonwealth of Massachusetts, through its state department of mental health, gave treatment a new status in the state by establishing psychiatric clinics in court houses. These were operated essentially as adjacent probation services, and some sixteen clinics now serve both adults and juveniles from approximately thirty of the state's judicial districts. The court-based clinic is still not presently the norm in the majority of the courts throughout the state. In general, however, where they do exist, these clinics are operated intelligently by men of considerable ability. As that aspect of the probation service improved, positions in the probation service became more professionally oriented with the setting of state-wide job standards in 1956 and a uniform salary scale in 1957. Thus we have approached a point where the Massachusetts probation officer will generally be a true and capable professional. Hopefully, there will not reoccur in any of our states the recent appointment in a neighboring state of a probation officer whose eight years experience working in a supermarket was accepted as equivalent to four years of college.

Massachusetts now, additionally, has a law through which our courts can relate to drug offenders, Chapter 889 of the Acts of 1969, the Comprehensive Drug Rehabilitation Program. Since this act has been in operation for only a few months at this writing, we do not know whether it will be a success. It is, however, another step in the developing desire for treatment for the drug addict and a departure from the primarily penal, hard-line approach that had been utilized in the past. Legislation offering civil commitment instead of criminal punishment was passed in New York and California. Then in 1966 the Congress passed the Narcotic Addict Rehabilitation Act (NARA). This act has been a failure because it is taking only those persons who are judged relatively sure to succeed in treatment. Any drug addict who is deemed unlikely to qualify is screened out of the program. Another major flaw is the extensive legal paperwork that must be done. An addict who may have been willing to go into the program on one day may have to wait for several weeks for the necessary approval in order to be sent to a federal treatment center for narcotics addicts such as that at Lexington, Kentucky. Then he is screened at the federal institution. Even after this lengthy process has been completed, addicts are generally returned as unsuitable for treatment. Recently commenced preliminary screenings in the addict's home community may improve this tortured process, but the act has a long way to go before becoming a credible weapon in the fight against drug abuse.

One hopes that the Massachusetts statute does not prove to have comparable defects. Under this law either an addict or drug-dependent person has the right to seek out treatment before the law seeks him out. Also, when a person who is charged with a drug offense for the first time is brought before the court, he has the right to request treatment. Even if he is charged with an offense not directly involving drugs, for example the kind of property offense that the heroin addict often must commit in order to obtain money to feed his addiction, the court may permit him this treatment alternative. This is not a perfect law: there are technical and possibly substantive problems with it. However, the significant point is that the law is moving in the right direction. Obviously we do not have an adequate number of treatment resources to meet the mandate of the law. When Professor Robert Hallgring of Northeastern University Law School and I completed the first real quantitative study of the drug abuse problem in the city of Boston in November 1969, one Boston paper headlined an editorial about our study: "4000 addicts and 22 beds." It was referring to our rather conservative estimate that there were approximately 4,000 addicts in the city of Boston at that time. The number is obviously significantly higher today. But one didn't have to estimate the number of beds. There were literally twenty-two beds in the City of Boston for the detoxification of addicts in the fall of 1969. Since then, the number of beds for detoxification has only gone up to thirty. While that is but one small aspect of treatment, it is, nevertheless, a major problem, and the Treatment Committee of Boston's Coordinating Council on Drug Abuse has been working in this and other areas. For the first time, we have had hospitals seeking a role that they can play.

A few comments about methadone are appropriate here. Methadone is an addicting synthetic narcotic. A doctor who prescribes methadone for more than the few days necessary to detoxify a person from heroin addiction, may be consciously addicting his patient to a narcotic drug. By no means should methadone maintenance be used for all persons, nor should there be any reflex action that says that persons in a given age group with a particular background will automatically get methadone; but methadone maintenance is too valuable a treatment approach when administered by competent and responsible physicians not to be a part of the drug program of any city experiencing appreciable heroin addiction. We must organize our resources so that there will be that kind of personal evaluation of care and treatment that will determine whether methadone blockade administered at an out-patient clinic with the individual remaining in the community or a residential treatment center or neighborhood storefront counselling is the best approach for that particular person. I think that all of these treatment modalities are encompassed by the realistic use of the word treatment, and our goal should be to make them all available. When we prematurely try to restrict the term "treatment," when we attempt to curry the favor of one or another of the advocates of the various types of treatment, we do a disservice to the persons whom we are ostensibly trying to help.

The Massachusetts statute defines treatment as services and programs for the care and rehabilitation of drug-dependent persons or persons in need of immediate assistance due to the use of a dependency-related drug. These services include, but are not limited to, medical, psychiatric, psychological, vocational, educational, and recreational programs. Treatment is not restricted to only one, or even several, of these services. This is a major policy commitment by the Commonwealth of Massachusetts. However, there still has been no comparable policy commitment at the federal level. There are some improvements in federal funding, and more apparently in the offing, and dedicated legislators like Senator Harold Hughes, chairman of the United States Senate Subcommittee on Alcoholism and Narcotics, will continue to work creatively and hard at this problem, as will individuals in the National Institute of Mental Health and elsewhere in the executive branch of the federal government. But we have yet to make the overall public commitment to the delivery of services needed to provide what at least in Massachusetts is now a legal right to which the individual is entitled. This is no longer a question of privilege. The defendant cannot be prosecuted if he is not accorded that legal right, and possibly the framing of the crisis in those blunt accurate terms will get more public response. Of course, the other alternative would be repealing or amending the statute. I hope that latter option will not be taken.

As a lawyer—as one who has taught criminal justice—I feel an obligation to speak about the law and its purposes. I call drug reform a law-and-order issue, because I regard the greatest problem in this country today the absence of rationality that has caused disrespect for the law. The failure to distinguish between one chemical substance and another, between one act and another, between marijuana and heroin, between an amphetamine and a barbiturate has contributed enormously to such disrespect. Narcotic drugs have been defined in some jurisdictions to include the hallucinogenic drugs and marijuana. How can there be respect for the law when we set forth a definition that we simply know is untrue? When we punish a violation involving marijuana on the same level as one involving a narcotic drug, we invite disregard for the current laws. Since 1966, when the Sandoz Pharmaceutical Company turned over its supply of quality-controlled LSD to the National Institute of Mental Health, we have left the manufacture of such substances to the basement chemist. The current cry of the Administration is to shut off the flow of the opiates into this country. I strongly favor that policy, but it isn't going to be the solution to the drug problem. Even if we had total cooperation of the hashish farmers in Turkey and a massive crackdown on the laboratories that are operating in southern France, that would not be enough. Synthetic drugs can be developed very quickly, and the basement chemist doubtless has turned up several new substances since this chapter was written.

I say it is time to take a fresh reappraisal of all of our legislation. It is time to undertake total recodifications of our drug laws. I personally believe that it is time to remove simple possession and use of marijuana from the criminal sphere. In evaluating a drug like marijuana we must be clear as to what the test for a regulated legalization should be. Is marijuana on trial in the sense that it must be proven safe beyond a reasonable doubt? Or should there be the same kind of standard that we have traditionally used in this country: that is, has marijuana been proven dangerous? Surely the latter approach is more appropriate and more honest. Marijuana has neither been proven always safe nor invariably dangerous. If we take a credible and straightforward approach to these facts in our drug-education programs, and if our society is willing to evaluate anew that basic question—what is a crime?—and then prescribe reasonable defensible penalties for those acts it deems criminal, our young people will respect the law.

I am afraid many of the good people working toward the common end of helping drug-dependent persons have great difficulty seeing the validity of views and approaches different from their own. I do not think we have reached the point yet where we can say one approach or even two will be all things for all people. We may never reach that stage. But we will develop new approaches and techniques. We must! Therefore, it is crucial that we make a monetary commitment at all levels of government to support the public policy pronouncements that have been made and will be made. We must open up more lines of communication so that people from many disciplines—both professionals and paraprofessionals, lawyers and police, judges and probation officers, physicians and psychiatrists, parents and children, and community workers—may know and respect one another. If we make such commitments and develop such processes of sharing and working together, we shall gain understanding and make some preliminary headway in dealing with the many drug users and drug offenders who are a part of our society. If drug abuse is permitted to accelerate for too much longer, we may find ourselves in the midst of an irreversible trend.

CHAPTER 5

THE STREET SYSTEM,
DRUGS, AND THE MILITARY SERVICE

THE STREET SYSTEM, DRUGS, AND THE MILITARY SERVICE[1]

BY HARVEY W. FELDMAN, PH.D.

The observations I will be making in this essay have been drawn from a field study of an Italian, working-class community in a large eastern city of the United States. The original intent was to examine the social features of drug-using behavior and, hopefully, to develop a conceptual scheme on how values, beliefs, and life-styles in the so-called "natural environment" underpin the origins and spread of drug use. The study began with the research question posed as follows: "What features in the social organization of the community made it fertile for the development of drug use among youth?" The study addressed itself primarily to the behavior of males.

In a previous article, I tried to suggest that young men in lower socioeconomic communities tailor their strivings for prestige and acceptance through efforts to compete and survive in street life. The qualities of excitement, feats of strength, and a multitude of risk-taking activities comprise the day-to-day props that make up the social interaction of what I refer to as the street system.

The street system, I believe, emerges out of the collective experience of low-income people, both youth and adults, to manage their lives within the context of an increasingly bureaucratic world that depends on an impersonal delivery of goods and services. Children grow up recognizing that both they and their parents are at the relative mercy of the representatives of bureaucratic systems. And whether the impersonality is the result of arbitrary treatment by a cruel individual or the consequence of complicated administrative

---

[1] This essay is based on data collected on a grant funded by the National Institute of Mental Health, Grant Number MH15281.

regulations, the results are the same: the individual situation is sub-ordinate to the smooth operations of the bureaucracy. As children—in my cases, young men—run through the institutional experiences either alone or with their parents they develop a heightened sense of their unimportance. In contacts with the schools, hospitals, police, courts, welfare, housing authorities, and the like, the course of inter-action is frequently a reminder that both they and their families are in inferior and/or powerless positions. The sense of worthlessness gets heightened if the person comes from an ethnic or racial group already encumbered with discrimination. But worse still is the youth or family whose special need has not been clarified in an administrative directive and requires individual handling.

As the youth develops his own life-experiences, observes those of his friends, listens to or watches those of his family, he learns that representatives of the important social institutions that impinge on his life (or on people like him) have defined him, under the most opti-mum conditions, as a burden to the smooth operations of their bu-reaucracy; or, as a near-person hardly worth the ink used to fill out the form that identifies him distinctly as an individual. The cumulative effects—and these assaults on his dignity occur with grinding regu-larity, especially for the young in the school system—lead the low-in-come youth to develop a double view of his social contract. On the one hand, he harbors a bitterness toward social institutions—sym-bolized by teachers and police—for triggering the events that place him in a demeaned position. On the other hand, he comes to view himself as the bureaucracy might view him: unworthy for better treat-ment, powerless, and unimportant to the bureaucratic system as any-thing more than a case or number.

One of the more important routes for young men in lower socio-economic neighborhoods to guard against assaults on their self-re-spect, to protect themselves from the corrosive damage to their sense of dignity, and to strive toward a self-image that merits recog-nition from others lies in their participation in a street system. One might say that the street system is a collective response to the ways social institutions diminish the self-images of young men in poor neighborhoods and assault their senses of dignity. As a result, the street system permits young men to participate in social activities where prestige and importance get determined by locally defined rules and unwritten bylaws that are independent of formal organizations.

I would like briefly to offer a summary of the quality of street life and its relationship to drug use. And even though the data may be sketchy, I would like to illustrate how the demands of the military experience might clash with the expectations of young men involved in both the street system and the drug experience.

For a large minority of males in lower socioeconomic neighborhoods, street life begins early. It may be identified for each individual as that point where the values of the street-corner group become more important as a guide to behavior than the teachings of his parents. Even in elementary-school years, boys begin seeking status positions among street friends and participate in activities that have embryonic features of toughness, daring, and a willingness to show bravery in the face of pain. These early street games, rather than emphasizing skills of coordination, test a youth's eagerness or reluctance to give and take brutal punishment. They are his first vivid demonstrations of courage in situations that chance injury.

As the boys grow into early adolescence, the excitement escalates to minor law-breaking activities such as joining friends in stealing cigarettes or vandalizing a school. The shared, forbidden activities become the bonds that tie youth together in a sense of solidarity. These activities may be viewed as "wrong" but they are almost never defined as "crime." Even when police become involved, the fun of escape for them seems more like an extension of street games than an example of the rising rate of delinquency.

As loyalty to peers grows stronger, parents unknowingly begin to lose their monopoly as agents of socialization. In carrying out his street activities, the youth must play a tricky secondary game of keeping information of his adventures from parents while trying to maximize public announcements of misdeeds among friends. As long as he does not get caught or apprehended, he may hold these two separate roles—street activist and dutiful son—without conflict.

The dual audience of parents and peers requires, however, a collusion of secrecy in which loyalty to street codes and street friends is pitted against conventional agents who might feed information to parents and disrupt the image he presents at home. Early in life, boys discover that "being a rat"—the act of divulging discrediting information to conventional socializing persons with authority to censure —is a violation of street confidentiality. In this light, the youths' commitment to street life becomes a search for trust among one another, both in carrying out exciting activities, as well as in sharing intimate knowledge about them. The rewards of mutually shared adventures and the earned trust among participating youth are evidently greatly satisfying. The loyalty is evidenced in those youth who move from the neighborhood but travel great distances to return daily to hang with friends on the corner or stand with them in the cold of a school yard.

While the rewards of trust are comforting, within the close network of friends, a dangerous undercurrent of competition makes group ranking an uncertainty. Youth attempt to stabilize their status, to make the responses of others more predictable, to bring some uniformity of expectation to street relationships. These efforts come in the form of *status assertions.* And status assertions appear in a variety of ways. The most common one is the verbal insult—called in the study neighborhood "ball-breaking"—and the most dramatic is fighting. Because of the special focus of the study, another important status assertion would be excessive drinking. In any case, the plan of action is to clarify a boy's position vis-à-vis his friends and hopefully in some observable way to enhance how others see him.

"BALL-BREAKING"

As the name of the activity indicates, the aim of "ball-breaking" is the reduction of someone's manly status carried out through insult or sarcastic humor. It is the gruff and frequently brutal counterpart to the middle-class "put-down." Rather than the ritualistic verbal interaction of "playing the dozens," where motherhood is the choice target, ball-breaking is spontaneous and attempts to magnify a person's weakness. In its cruder form, the verbal attack is simply name-calling; and the names selected always have a negative local meaning. The way in which the intended victim deals with the ball-breaking attempt—whether he retaliates with counter statements of equal or superior verbal agility, becomes embarrassed, or loses his temper—will determine the manner of deference his friends show him. Within a verbal situation, ball-breaking pastimes become demonstrations of who controls any given situation through abilities of phrasing, timing, or selection of invidious names. Ball-breaking can be mild, clever, or harshly insulting, depending on the situation, the creativity of the individuals or the status of the participants. The main point of ballbreaking is that a young man's street position in the hierarchy of social types may rise or fall to the degree to which he can make others objects of ball-breaking and exempt himself.

The impact of being the central figure in a game where the goal is humiliating a person by forcing into public view personal and painful shortcomings, of becoming for brief or long periods an unwilling clown, is a bitter experience youth would prefer to avoid.

FIGHTING

In the street life of the study neighborhood, no personal quality is more respected than toughness. It is one of the major, and in some cases the single, individual feature upon which a high-status street reputation is built. Toughness, however, is an abstract concept, and for the designation to be associated with a particular youth, claims to toughness must be demonstrated in some observable way. Athletics, especially games like football, where excellence is determined by the manipulation of physical strength, provide one route. A youth can show he possesses qualities of fearlessness, determination, and physical coordination by the way in which he tackles or blocks his opposition. While these athletic skills are respected among the youth in the study neighborhood, they lose their glitter if the same qualities are not transferred to the street where the basic unit for the proof of toughness is the fight.

For the youth set on winning respect and deference in the streets, he must realize that fighting is one of the principal instruments. One youth observed the widespread acceptance of this dictum when he described himself in relation to street life in the following manner:

You'd be surprised. You grow up in certain areas and they become values. You know, who could steal the most, who could fight the best and they become like *normal* values. You know because you just merely adjust to the environment. These were the values that all your friends appreciate. (Would you say that it was a way to get status?) Yes. The one that could fight the best was looked up to. In other words, like all my desires were to fight a lot when I was young. It was the accepted thing because, you know, obviously I looked around and saw the ones that were looked up to the most and respected were the tough guys. That's what I craved.

Two important aspects set the stage for individual fights: the social setting of peers whose opinions are the basis of a youth's social ranking, and some initiating gesture or comment that threatens to lower that social position. The consequences of the lowered position have repercussions beyond the incident itself. For a youth in the study neighborhood to permit someone of lower (or even equal) status to "insult" him, according to street etiquette, raises the question of whether his claim to the status position he holds is completely merited. Failure to respond with appropriate action has the potential of opening the door to innumerable future attempts from other youth jockeying for a higher street ranking. Not only will more people consider themselves eligible to "break his balls," but the quality of content may become more degrading and the intensity of insult may increase.

Still, fighting is less frequent than the amount of talk about it would indicate. In more middle-class areas of the study city or in the memories of yesterday, a fight between two boys may have been something of a boxing match, if not carried out strictly according to the Marquis of Queensberry rules, at least with some gentlemanly understanding that an opponent knocked down be permitted to rise before being hit again. In the study neighborhood, the stakes of the game were higher, and the risk of injury considerably greater. Frequently, fighting involved use of hands, cleated shoes, chains, knives, and, on occasion, guns. Since fighting has the potential of triggering far more violent results than the precipitating incident apparently merits —and where severe bodily injury may be only an insulting word away—hesitancy about pursuing a conflicting situation becomes understandable.

DRINKING

It is significant that even at the time of the study, most respondents reported that their first experience with a drug-induced intoxication was not with marijuana but with alcohol. Few respondents reported light, social drinking and stated that even very early drinking had one clear objective: to get high. Almost all respondents described three significant components to their drinking: (1) it was initiated within the peer group, (2) the aim was to get drunk, and (3) the side effects of sickness, vomiting, dizziness, and the hangover syndrome were memorable and distasteful byproducts. In the face of anticipated physical misery, these ordeals of drinking and the subsequent suffering become the occupational hazards in securing a street reputation. When compared to fighting, however, getting drunk as a method of declaring a claim for respect does not place the youth in danger of physical injury in quite the sudden, dramatic way a street brawl might. Because parental and legal prohibitions make adolescent drinking a form of risk-taking, although a mild one, it could act as a minimal selling point to all observers that a declaration to the code of the streets had been issued. With other street boys as witnesses, a youth can demonstrate that he has flaunted prohibitions of law and family rule by daring an act denied him by reason of his age. He does not need to possess special qualities of physical strength; he does not have to pit his skill and muscle against someone else's, where defeat or victory might lower or raise his standing. He need only have an orientation toward impressing his friends, the determination and endurance to force down sufficient amounts of alcohol and then wait for the intoxicating effects. Drinking, in brief, is a street game anyone can play.

LOCAL SOCIAL TYPES

The way in which a youth manages street challenges of fighting, "ball-breaking," drinking, and other forms of action behavior adds up to the sum total of his character as evaluated and judged by other local youth. As he grows older, these tests become part of the repertoire of activities that begin to divide a youth's loyalties between insiders and outsiders. Youth who declare (through their actions) loyalty to the street become insiders, and the symbol of societal opposition is epitomized by the police. Loyalty to friends upheld in the face of personal disadvantages (such as arrests, police brutality, etc.) contribute to the prestige youth strive toward. If the tests for gaining entry have been successfully passed, even on a minimal basis, the youth is designated a "solid guy." He may have failings, but his main characteristic is that he can be trusted by other insiders even though he may hold low social ranking within the street status scheme. In group actions, the "solid guy" can be depended on for support in illegal activities, defenses against outsiders, and pledged to an informal code of secrecy from parents and police. In the study neighborhood, all aspirants to the "solid guy" role can be charted on a continuum from low to high status and get locally defined by the following: (1) "faggot," (2) "asshole" or "jerk," (3) "solid guy" (garden variety), (4) "tough guy," and (5) "crazy guy."

"Faggots" constitute the lowest ranking in the status hierarchy. The designation does not refer to any homosexual aberration but merely to the individuals' inability to manage manly actions. They are either physically weak or display inordinate fears. Most frequently, they hang at the fringes of the street group. Often they preserve conforming moral standards, and their attempts to participate in the rough-and-tumble activities of the street cause more laughter than respect. Their outstanding feature is an inability to protect themselves from verbal or physical abuse from others. In attempting to ward off becoming the focus of group "ball-breaking," they usually offer a submissive defense that is interpreted by others as "silly," "stupid," or "dumb." Unsure of themselves physically, they receive physical punishment without attempts at retaliation. Some members see the person in the "faggot" status as merely the object of a time-consuming joke, the topic around which amusing stories revolve. With other members, he is a focal point of anger and directed hostility. Occasionally, higher status members show concern or express guilt about actions and statements made against the person in the "faggot" status. These infrequent offers of protection, plus the individual's desire to cling to the fragments of friendship he finds in the group, provide the few thin threads that make him a group member.

The status of "asshole" or "jerk" is similarly low, but not as low as "faggot." It is more a temporary designation, situationally induced. He may have put himself in a position where someone of equal status has outwitted him or reduced his manly claims. His failure to take action against an offender, to accept humiliation without recourse to violence, diminishes the respect others might otherwise grant him. Under such circumstances, the individual becomes a figure of scorn because he either permits "someone to make an asshole out of him" or "acts like a jerk" when more aggressive actions are expected. In recounting these situations, if a youth claims a stance of toughness when he had in fact acted less aggressively—either exaggerating or lying about his defense of self—and his pretense to toughness gets unmasked, the status of "asshole-jerk" may become a more permanent street label.

Avoiding these derogatory designations in the early years of adolescence becomes a struggle for each male, and he must master his inner fears of personal injury. Failing this, he learns to accept the ridicule that comes with low-status ranking. Because the designations of "faggot," "asshole," and "jerk" are stinging attacks on his total character and may well determine the quality of respect (or lack of it) from his peer group, and knowing that these relationships will last into adult life, the majority of street youths strive painstakingly to avoid becoming placed in these low-status categories. A boy on the streets has only two choices: avoiding contact with local street youth, or acting more in conformity with local demands of toughness. Either course becomes perilous and sets in motion high tension levels.

The middle-ground position has no locally designed label, and I have called a youth in this status position simply "solid guy" (garden variety). He has sufficient qualities of strength or daring to enable him to manage all other youth on the "faggot-asshole-jerk" level. He may lack physical qualities of coordination or strength which would help him rise to a higher position in the status hierarchy. His willingness to chance daring behavior or to fight bigger and stronger opponents, even though losing is inevitable, demonstrates his courage. In the language of the street, he "has balls," which means that he exerts his rights in situations persons of lesser status would accept. He has, however, an intelligent understanding of the social order of "solid guy" types and avoids circumstances that would pit him against the "tough guy" or "crazy guy."

"Tough guys," for the most part, meet and pass local tests of strength with a minimum of effort and seem to have natural physical qualities of speed, stamina, and tenacity. They frequently fight opponents who are three or four years older or opponents whose high status has been generally recognized. In doing so, they develop a street reputation when they perform respectably or, in some outstanding cases, actually win. Some "tough guys" search out situations that enhance their street reputations, bringing with them an audience of friends who take the core truth and embroider folktales of their strength. Others prefer a less conflictful existence than their followers thrust on them. What holds true, in either case, is the determination to avoid being considered an "asshole" or "jerk" in any situation that can be clarified with a fight.

A step beyond the "tough guy" is the "crazy guy," someone who conscientiously strives for a reputation that extorts fear and respect for his capacity to fight with such ferocity and brutality that inflicting physical pain or injury on his victims has little concern for him. His terms of battle are unconditional surrender and total victory in which he uses whatever means he has available: knives, broken bottles, bricks, lead pipes, pool cues, guns. Although his face-to-face relationships may be restricted to his own street-corner group, stories of his actions become widespread. Within the "solid guy" hierarchy, the "crazy guy" earns the highest prestige. It should not be assumed, however, that the "crazy guy" is necessarily psychiatrically ill. Rather than a distorted view of "reality," his understanding of local expectations and practices is frequently brutally accurate. He recognizes that violent action is a route to respect, and then conscientiously, even rationally, maps out tactics of aggression. Such actions are carried off for their maximum dramatic effect and are calculated to provide lurid details upon which a "crazy" reputation may be steadily built. Over the years, he has battled and earned the fear/respect due him; and his biography could be told by the scars he has accumulated. The toll it has taken can be charted in what seems to be an almost ridiculous series of arrests and incarcerations.

Yet, the "crazy guy" has a unique sociological function within the street system. To the individuals who surround him, his apparent disregard of danger to himself gives him an air of heroism, a sense of being slightly larger than life. By the time his reputation as "crazy" has been secured, he may have survived one or two stabbings himself or have been on the receiving end of a shooting and have converted injury into victory. His capacity to make others yield to his will, to dominate a troublesome situation and conclude it on his own terms by means of terror, strikes a note of envy in the inner world of wish fulfillment of street boys who too often feel that fate, bad luck, or fault of character makes them inevitable losers. From the viewpoint of the street youth, the "crazy guy" never seems to know defeat. He manipulates situations to his liking; he appears to control the course of his own destiny. As a hero, he is no distant gladiator performing in Madison Square Garden. He is local and his victories have proximity. For young men growing up in a neighborhood where the code of the streets makes toughness and risk-taking a necessity, these top-level "solid guys" are symbolic of the latent belief that with enough daring, enough masculine confidence, enough "balls," an individual, even one with humble physical qualifications, can master a threatening environment. And the need for such local heroes is evidenced by the way in which tales of his exploits are exaggerated.

TENSION LEVELS AND THE "SOLID GUY"

One of the serious byproducts of behavior that flirts with violence, violations of law, and a life-style that produces in the time it takes to throw a punch instant victors and victims is that, carried out day-by-day, participants live lives, not of quiet desperation, but ones in which the stomach juices churn constantly. People on guard against being the butt of a local con-game, who feel the loss of prestige and status at any minute, or who live under the threat that an embarrassing or humiliating incident may brand them in the eyes of their friends as "assholes" or "jerks" or "faggots" live in a chronic state of preparedness for conflict. Their tension level remains high. Tension, then, becomes a natural state of being. And the youth involved in the everyday affairs of the street hardly recognizes the inner disquiet as tension. Evidence of it shows in nail biting, stammering, picking at open sores, and often blunt expressions that life in the neighborhood "sucks." A great number of youths live with constant anxiety as though each new encounter has the potential of erupting into a major confrontation. Under conditions where large numbers of youth and young adults lived daily with these unspecified anxieties, the social climate was conducive not only to new forms of action but was attuned to activities that might alter a personal feeling-state of tension.

It is significant that in the neighborhood under study the first reported drug used on a widespread basis was a cough syrup with a heavy codeine component. While the earliest stages of drug experimentation in the study neighborhood are historically clouded, what seems overwhelmingly clear is that the first wave of drug users were high-status "solid guys" with local reputations of either "tough" or "crazy."

I will not detail how these early discoverers pioneered the various drug substances other than to point out that as leaders in the street system the very fact of their involvement in drugs made the activity a form of action fascination for a large number of "solid guys" eager to latch onto a new and reckless fad. And because the drug experience provides a pleasurable feeling-state, the sum total of the activity made an almost perfect match for the life-style of the street system. It had components of illegality to provide adventure. Young men could demonstrate their loyalties to one another in dramatic exhibits of silence. The risk to body and life inherent in ingesting a foreign or unknown substance could illustrate daring and risk. And the final payoff was frequently a condition of well-being, often too ecstatic for verbal description.

THE MILITARY SERVICE

I suspect that there was a time in our modern history when the kinds of young men I have described would have been ideal candidates for the military service. Their search for adventure, their love of excitement, their pleasure in fighting, their willingness even to die as a way of becoming after death the kind of hero they know is valued on the street, seems tailored to a war machine. But in the days of the Vietnam war, a new kind of cynicism about military service has emerged, not only among the resentful middle-class youth who view this particular war as illegal without the consent of Congress, but also among the dependable working-class youth who have traditionally volunteered their bodies and angers amidst patriotic slogans and sentimental farewell parties. If the young men involved in my study are representative, there appears to be among the stable working-class youth a growing dissatisfaction with the responsibilities of military service. Some of these dissatisfactions have their roots in drug-associated behavior and other dissatisfactions seem more connected to the mismatch between street aspirations for status (based on glory) and the requirements of the military to wage a war of attrition where the military goal appears to be a body count rather than the more traditional objective of land acquisition. The very nature of the war-style has raised serious questions among many of the working-class youth in the study area regarding the utility of military service as a route to gaining prestige in the civilian world of street life.

Prior to my beginning the study in 1968, a number of street influentials had already served some short or long period of military service and had come home. Almost without exception their military experience had been less than beneficial to them, both during the years of service and on their return to the community. These experiences, especially for the top level "solid guys," were discussed, almost always bitterly, so that lesser street youth developed a sour outlook as a prejudgment of what military service would probably be like. In many cases, their subsequent military careers provided supportive evidence to what they had been told. I noted a distinct difference, for example, between the stories the veterans of my generation told and those of the young men from the Vietnam experience. And the major difference was that my generation tended to screen out negative experiences and remember the *good* times while these young men minimized the benefits of military service and chose to speak almost exclusively of the incidents they hated, underscoring where possible the ubiquity and intensity of the evils, deceptions, and hypocrisies they witnessed.

For some young men, the entry point into the military is non-voluntary, frequently a form of punishment delivered by either the court system or the draft board. It is not uncommon for judges in district courts, especially in lower socioeconomic neighborhoods, because of an absence of civilian facilities perhaps, to suggest—which is tantamount to a court sentence—that enlistment in the military be considered an acceptable punishment in lieu of jail. This tactic seems to be a carry-over from the old English judicial system which helped the navy, especially, to maintain its enlistment quotas. Today, in America, it may also serve a similar purpose but has the added motive of removing one "trouble maker"—according to those who staff the court—from both the street and the court system. Just how young men who enter military service through this route fare may be the basis for future research. At present, to the best of my knowledge at least, there has been no systematic study made. The young men I have spoken with have, almost without exception, run into difficulty and have been discharged early in their military careers under less than honorable circumstances. Some of them, in fact, were the early pioneers of the drug sub-system in the study neighborhood.

Another non-voluntary route comes through a form of punishment at the draft boards or induction centers. Evidently there are persons staffing these operations, either under official directives or with a patriotic fervor, who view any physically firm young man not eager to surrender two or more years of his life as a likely candidate to be punished via military service. When drug use is involved, the situation becomes more opaque. Indications or direct statements by young

73

men of their unsuitability for the military are considered less than valid, as the following quote from a tape-recorded interview with a male respondent demonstrates:

> So that day I went there [induction physical]. I was stoned. I said, "I'm going to make them throw me out. I ain't going." So, I was stoned. The guy [staff] didn't want to hear nothing. He was passing me on every test. I couldn't even see the board. He'd say, "Read the chart." I could hardly see it. He says, "All right, you pass." I says, "Pass? I didn't even say it yet." They just took, they didn't know nothing. I guess they done it for spite. They knew I was trying to get out.

If the rest of the military experience had been a reversal of the beginning, it would have read like a John Wayne movie where the reluctant recruit slowly sees the blessings of the corps and ends the scenario in some heroic act in combat. In this case, however, the young man received, after an investment of staff time, mainly from the medical branch of the army, an undesirable discharge. Presently, he is serving a jail sentence on a drug-related conviction.

The failure of appropriate screening, of drawing unqualified personnel into the service, seems to have laid the groundwork for a transfer of the drug sub-system from civilian life into the military. Once into the military, young men from similar working-class backgrounds tend to collect together, not by any "natural" inclination but through planned action. And the army policy of punishing drug violators appears to provide one form of publicity necessary to identify drug users to one another. As one respondent in the air force claimed: "Some guys got busted, you know, for smoking pot. So, I started, you know, 'Wow, here we are.' You know, 'Junkies in the service. I finally met my kind. Let me go talk to these dudes.'"

Much has been said recently of drug use in the war zone of Vietnam, but I know of no study directed to the analysis of how drugs function to reduce the tension levels of men in combat areas, in much the same way drugs function in neighborhoods where reputations are built through risk-taking. According to my limited discussion with respondents who served in Southeast Asia, the comparisons of tension have a similarity, but with one very important difference. In the street system, violence is connected to settling disputes between men, carried out under unwritten rules that bind the combatants to injure only those persons connected to the core of the dispute. In Vietnam, any Oriental, so I am told by some of the returning veterans, is a potential enemy, and punishing civilians—including women and children—whose loyalties are ambiguous does not seem to fit the picture of honor street youth have been socialized to respect. In World War II, at least according to the war films young men of this generation see on the late show, the enemies were men, fought hand-to-hand, or rifle-to-rifle, but under a code only the enemy would violate, such as employing old people, taking innocent hostages, destroying civilian homes, or, most horrifying of all, killing or maiming defenseless children. The experiences of the combat veterans of Vietnam with whom I have spoken have indicated they manage their own violations of this code in one of two ways: (1) they view all Vietnamese as potential enemies, and justify their own brutality in a street system style of defense: "I got him (them) before they got me,"—and it might be useful research to find in what magnitude and what depth, or (2) they come to identify themselves as possessing a strange mixture of irrational brutality and patriotic zeal, which frightens them. I know of one marine veteran of four and a half years of service, part of which was served in Vietnam, who was unable to neutralize or forget his own acts of violence against women and children and these recurring confessions were made to me at least a year before publicity on the My Lai incident. His experimentation with heroin, a rather strong tension reducer, may well have been his treatment alternative to a continual sense of war guilt and confusion rather than the help through psychiatry he spoke of seeking so often. He died, so I am told, in a furnished room in Maine where he had gone as an escape from heroin. The facts are not clear, but he was found in his bedroom with an empty bottle of methadone he had gotten from a doctor for withdrawal. Evidently, he had vomited and died as the result of asphyxiation. Both suicide and homocide were considered in the investigation, I am told, but for those of us who knew and heard him speak of his war experiences—acts he clearly defined as crimes if they were performed in the street system of his home neighborhood—may cause us to infer that one solution to what he called "crazy feelings" was to mask them with drugs. Military researchers might explore the ways and undercurrents these internal Nuremberg trials erode the sense of honor and eat away at strivings to maintain a constructive view of self.

Space does not permit me to raise questions on the struggles some veterans face when returning to neighborhoods where a drug sub-system contains a large portion of friends left behind. The veterans I knew, naturally, had become drug users either prior to their military service, during, or after it. I am sure there were other veterans who did not become involved with drugs, but they were outside the present scope of my study. For those who became involved with drugs and were caught by the authorities, I noted that a favorable war record was of little benefit in receiving help with a drug problem. In fact, one young marine who had been seriously wounded in Vietnam was arrested for "being present where a narcotic drug was found." He himself admitted to beginning heroin use, perhaps twice before he was arrested. He was placed on $25,000 bail, a figure he claimed was higher than the bail given to the big shots of the Mafia. He was committed to a maximum security hospital for observation, and subsequently placed on two-years' probation. At no time did his military service record act as a point of leverage in a reduced sentence; and no one, not even he, suggested treatment for drug use at a veterans' hospital, even though he had been released from one only a few months prior to the drug arrest.

Either through neglect or design, we have permitted a drug problem to grow. We have structured a system of cure based almost solely on punishment of individual users (and have developed an explanation of cause consistent with the punishment). With regard to the military, the civilian sector has dumped the drug problem on the services, believing, perhaps, that its special brand of discipline will in some inexplicable fashion remake young men already tailored for a street system. The military, in turn, a bit too smug about its potential for character reformation, has concluded that it cannot incorporate intoxicating substances other than alcohol into its mores or remove the punishment from its code of military justice. As a result, it has, in turn, dumped the problem back onto the civilian sector. Together, both the military and the civilian world have colluded to provide young men with war-time experiences that have apparently scrambled our society's moral order—and this includes the moral ideologies of the street system. Without a well-formulated plan of treatment that demonstrates to young men that their society has concern for their health and well-being—both in the military and out of it, without a significant alteration in administrative policies to permit drug users to escape criminal designations, without a thorough revamping of our outmoded drug laws that have little relationship to a scientific understanding of the problem, the projected course of the relationship between a large segment of our youthful population and their government will be, I think, one of collision; or one of disparate directions in which young men grow increasingly cynical in their belief that bureaucratic efforts and political decisions get made, not on the citizens' behalf, but for the gain or profit of men in power.

The young men among whom I gathered my data have, for the most part, acted in good faith with their government. They may have made mistakes—and many of them accept an archaic form of punishment for those mistakes far better than you or I would—but they still continue to strive toward a stance of individual dignity, whether they use drugs or not. I think the goal of any effort to grapple with the drug situation must understand that the root causes lie not in the pathology of individual users, nor in the violent quality of life in the street system, but quite clearly in the relationships between individuals and the social institutions that play such an important part in shaping the sense of self, which we call an identity. Each social institution has the responsibility to examine its own social function. The task of the military, as I see it, would be to provide experiences that promote a respectable sense of self and not to confine itself solely to training young men in the instruments of war.

I would like to underscore that my comments on the interrelationships between drug use and military service have not been based on a direct study within the military system. They came from retrospective comments of young men who had spent time in one of the services. None of them blamed their military service as the *cause* of their turn to drugs, even though they admitted that access to drugs compared favorably to their civilian experience. Perhaps more indirectly, they raised questions on how the military experience reinforced the aspects of their street ideology that were based on the manipulation of violence. The impact of the military tour of duty on youths' conceptions of their private moral order should be more closely examined by our psychologists and sociologists in order to understand the effects of clear training directives for war, like the one a marine veteran claimed his platoon sergeant gave, "Remember," my ex-marine respondent quoted his sergeant as saying, "You ain't nothing but a hired killer."

DRUG ABUSE:
THE CRIMINALIZATION OF
A SOCIAL-HEALTH PROBLEM

CHAPTER **6**

DRUG ABUSE:
THE CRIMINALIZATION OF
A SOCIAL-HEALTH PROBLEM[1]
BY DAVID E. JORANSON, M.S.W.

America's policy toward drugs is destructive. Based more upon punitive moral convictions than on sound information, it ignores totally the fundamental nature of drug abuse, *in reality a health and social problem.* Because of our harsh and repressive policies, we are now confronted with a stunning array of tangential crises. Here are some of them:

Thousands of young people who are users rather than purveyors have been dealt criminal punishment. National data from the U.S. Government publication *Crime in the United States* shows that between 1960 and 1969, Narcotic Drug Law violations by juveniles increased 2453 percent, reflecting primarily a high prevalence of increased marijuana arrests.

The drug problem in Vietnam has seen possibly the most punitive handling to date. Arrests for use and possession of heroin by Vietnam servicemen were 250 in 1969, 1,146 in 1970, and 1,084 in the first *quarter* of 1971. In the past two years, 11,000 servicemen have been less than honorably discharged for drug related offenses, making them ineligible for Veterans Administration benefits.

Users of drugs to the extent that they have a critical health problem have few, if any, places to go for help. They are not likely to expose themselves to arrest and prosecution. Because the abuse of drugs has been viewed historically as a legal matter, the medical pro-

---

[1] Reprinted with permission from *Washington Bulletin* (Washington, D.C.: Social Legislation Information Service), Vol. 22, Issue 12 (June 28, 1971). An earlier version appeared as "America's Drug Policies: Killer or Cure" in *Wisconsin Alumnus,* March 1971.

fession's access to the user is sharply limited and medical facilities are inappropriate and inadequate. Research into the cause and treatment of drug abuse has been stultified.

Communities, hysterical about the drug issue, are wasting great effort and resources. Community planning activities proceed at a crisis pace as though there were an epidemic. Community "experts" abound. Drug committees are everywhere. Youth in many schools have been subjected increasingly to a form of amateur, irrelevant "drug education" which ignores the abuse of legal drugs and solidifies negative feelings toward adults and adult attitudes on drugs.

Myths and stereotypes about drugs have further alienated youth. The public sees a direct connection between drug use and the other generation gap issues—radicalism, "permissiveness," rebellion. This further complicates efforts to approach drug use with reason and understanding. The development by youth of their own informal resources for drug problems is an example of the polarity that has resulted.

Illegal drug traffic is largely responsible for the prosperity of organized crime which capitalizes both on national policies and individual problems. Organized crime is able to flourish as it does because it provides wanted services: gambling, prostitution, and drugs. The high risks involved in marketing illegal drugs drive up the price so that the addict must resort to crime in order to support his dependency. (The syndicate converts stolen goods or prostitution pay into the cash the addict needs to pay it for expensive drugs.) According to the National Institute of Mental Health, society's cost of supporting organized crime in narcotics abuse alone amounts to $541 million annually. This amounts to a tax-free, tacit conspiracy between our policies and crime, with the addict and the public caught in the squeeze.

Yet rather than abandon the use of the criminal sanction the federal government gives $1 million to Mexico for an impossible program to eradicate marijuana. This results in a decrease in the marijuana supply and the consequent influx of more dangerous drugs, tending to confine the supply market still more to organized crime. In the context of our drug-oriented culture it may be that sensational media coverage and scare drug programs function inadvertently as the advertising and promotional arm of organized crime.

Law enforcement efforts often include conduct which many consider to be more reprehensible than the target behavior. There is considerable feeling against such methods as illegal search and seizure, entrapment, improper arrest, electronic surveillance, abuse of the informant system, the no-knock entry. Officials who profess to be "tough on crime" clog the courts with drug-use charges against youngsters or members of minority groups, aware that the ensuing publicity will convince the public that law enforcement is handling the problem effectively.

MARIJUANA POLICY

If we can assume that laws are based on utilitarian principles of protecting public health and welfare, most citizens would correctly deduce from the law that the weed is, in fact, highly dangerous. Indeed, the rationale behind the Marijuana Tax Act of 1937—the federal prohibition of marijuana—was that it caused immorality and violence. Acts of violence and vice being among the most offensive to society, it then seemed reasonable to end use of the drug by relying on the deterrent effect of heavy penalties. It was an expensive move: enforcement, trials and incarceration cost the public money, but we have accepted the burden. When we read of the arrest, prosecution and jailing of marijuana users, we feel secure in the knowledge that the law is operating as intended.

But the law of the land may be used in ways which are *not* practical or reasonable. Policy is often developed by powerful special interest groups on their own behalf. Laws can be used to censor those whose life styles conflict with ours. It's happened before in our nation's history. A good example was Prohibition—the "marijuana issue" of the 1930's.

The enactment of Prohibition has been interpreted by authorities —one among them Joseph Gusfield in his book *Symbolic Crusade*— as a censorship of the life-style and behavior of urban Catholics by white rural Protestants. Catholicism, "city life," and alcohol were viewed by the WASPs as a threat to the moral fabric of their society. They focused their energies on the dangers of drinking, and succeeded in making it illegal. Thus, with Protestant morality upheld, who could doubt that urban Catholics were of less value in American society. Only when it became clear that the law was not a deterrent to use of liquor while it damaged the lives of thousands, made gangsters rich, and remained unenforceable, Prohibition was repealed.

The circumstances surrounding today's prohibition of marijuana are remarkably like that event in our history. As in the days of Prohibition, millions of Americans ignore the law, and illegal use of the drug is widespread. Young people are serving prison sentences for having been caught. Many indignant citizens say this is as it should be—that marijuana is dangerous to society, its illegality reasonable.

Yet the assumption that the law is based on fact is erroneous. Whatever the marijuana laws are, they are *not* accurate statements about the dangers of the drug. The fact of the matter is that as far as science has been able to determine, the danger potential for most individuals is less from marijuana than from our two national pacifiers, alcohol and cigarettes. Marijuana does not produce physical dependence. It does not cause the tissue damage and disease directly associated with alcohol and tobacco. Psychological dependence may occur with marijuana as with all mind-altering substances. Today, the greatest danger in marijuana use lies in violating the law. The "cure" is worse than the disease.

Our concern must be that dangerous substances should not be freely available to youngsters, or those who are unstable or prone to drug dependence. *Control* is the issue, not legality.

John Kaplan, in his book *Marijuana: The New Prohibition*, points out that the assumption that marijuana is linked with violent crime was used to persuade Congress of the need for outlawing the drug. Several years of campaigning by the Federal Bureau of Narcotics culminated in the prohibition of marijuana.

"How many murders, suicides, robberies, criminal assaults, holdups, burglaries, and deeds of maniacal insanity (marijuana) causes each year, especially among the young, can only be conjectured," testified the commissioner of the Bureau of Narcotics. Indeed, every case history gathered by the bureau in evidence illustrated the violent and immoral effects of the drug.

It must have required a good imagination and a certain moral persuasion to be convinced by this "evidence." Never was there an effort made to demonstrate a causal relationship between marijuana and violence or immorality. According to Kaplan, one typical testimony used by the bureau proclaimed: "A citizen of Alamosa, Colorado, stated that there had been scores of cases of violent and petty crimes and insanity in southern Colorado in recent years incited by the use of marijuana. Local officials there have been seriously aroused about the problem."

It was on such statements that Congress criminalized a virtually unknown drug without opposition.

Harry J. Anslinger, now almost eighty years old, once assistant commissioner of Prohibition (an interesting fact in itself) and subsequently commissioner of the Federal Bureau of Narcotics for thirty-three years, is generally considered to have been most responsible for the federal prohibition of marijuana. He believed, and according to recent statements still does, that marijuana is used by the psychologically and socially maladjusted, that it causes violence, and that it is an aphrodisiac. In reading his remarks one is struck by the intensity of his views and the minor role scientific knowledge about drugs plays in forming his judgments.[2] It is on such scientifically hollow generalizations that we've been raised[3]; it's on them that we generally concur with the country's drug policies. It's on them that we've turned a health problem into a legal cause (lately including the newer psychedelics) and delegated enforcement to the Federal Bureau of Narcotics.

Given our historic tradition which, generally speaking, allows the morality of those in power to be expressed through the law, the phenomenon of our drug policies can be described as having ethnocentric qualities—one group believing in the superiority of its ways and tending to reject the behavior and values of other groups having different practices and beliefs. Thus our drug laws are based upon austere and rigid concepts of right and wrong, accompanied by a

---

[2] See, for example, his comments in "Playboy Panel: The Drug Revolution," *Playboy* Magazine (February 1970).

[3] It is worth noting that some *current* drug research is also scientifically hollow. In the April 19, 1971 issue of the *Journal of the American Medical Association* appeared a widely publicized study by two physicians who concluded that for 38 patients marijuana had led to "serious psychological effects, sometimes complicated by neurologic signs and symptoms." An examination of this research reveals no scientific basis for the conclusions. They use the same fallacious reasoning ("post hoc, ergo propter hoc") that allowed Anslinger to draw his conclusions that marijuana leads to crime and heroin. It is unfortunate that the efforts applied to the widespread publicity of the study were not instead applied to the scientific rigor. It is even more unfortunate that such a study appeared in a learned journal.

fear of loss of self-control and a tight-lipped conviction that pleasure must be earned. Within this context of ethnocentric and Puritan policy-making (the ideology which forms the very heart of cultural and racial discrimination in this country), it is no surprise that the people who used marijuana in 1936 before passage of the Marijuana Tax Act were largely members of minority groups.

NARCOTICS POLICY

In 1914 Congress enacted the Harrison Act to control legitimate drug traffic. This was its only function and it has been largely effective. Nevertheless, through some interpretations of this act plus several decisions by the U.S. Supreme Court, the Narcotics Division of the Treasury Department (which later became the Federal Bureau of Narcotics and is now the Bureau of Narcotics and Dangerous Drugs), with the cooperation of the American Medical Association, removed the treatment of addicts from the medical profession. For some time after the Harrison Act was passed the medical profession was attempting to contribute to the understanding of addiction. But there were some irresponsible physicians who drew much criticism in regard to their prescription of narcotics in the course of treatment. Thus the AMA requested an interpretation of the act to prevent doctors from using drugs in the course of therapy. The Narcotics Division, through two Supreme Court decisions against physicians who had abused their license to prescribe drugs (*Webb* v *US* [1919], and *US* v *Behrman* [1922]) was able to suppress effectively the treatment of addicts by medical practitioners. The prosecution of physicians for treating addicts and the closing of the admittedly poorly administered addiction clinics brought about an interpretation of heroin addiction as primarily a legal problem.

The effect has been to make the addict a criminal by forcing him out of society to deal with organized crime in order to support his habit. Given the high cost of goods and services in the underworld, the addict must usually resort to crime—robbery, hustling, prostitution—in order to pay for drugs. Moreover, he is subject to overdoses, disease, and impure or diluted heroin, and often has to withdraw "cold turkey" in a jail cell. Even the use of the term "addict," with its emotion-laden connotations, removes the problems of drug dependency from the realm of reason. Our laws and attitudes have made the drug-dependent person unemployable, have seriously threatened his health, and have generally labeled him somewhat less than human in the eyes of society.

PRESIDENT'S ADVISORY COUNCIL
ON EXECUTIVE ORGANIZATION

This council which was established by the President was charged with a broad review of the organization of the executive branch of the Government. The President named Roy L. Ash Chairman of the Council and its members were selected from outstanding leaders in business and Government. After eighteen months of intensive study and analysis, the Council concluded that the current departmental structure for domestic programs was not adapted to the needs of Government in the seventies. Acting on this conclusion, it urged a restructuring of the existing departments based on the organizing principle of the major purposes served.

The Ash Council's recommendation was added to a long list of studies by distinguished task forces and commissions which have urged the reorganization of the domestic departments and a strengthening of departmental management.

Few are aware of a report from the Ash Council. Reportedly its recommendations dealt with drug abuse as symptomatic of other ills, and pointed out the need to change drug policies and to centralize drug abuse responsibility in the federal government. The report was submitted, but my personal efforts and those of the office of a U.S. Congressman have been unsuccessful in obtaining a copy. We have found that no one officially connected with it will discuss it.

VIETNAM

One wonders if the President needed to wait until 40,000 servicemen became heroin-dependent before he was galvanized into creating a separate federal agency to implement a crash program of treatment. There is no question that heroin dependence has long been with us, particularly among struggling minorities in the nation's beleaguered inner cities. The solution for them was prison, because those who made the laws never dreamed that their own kind could become "addicts."

Government officials would now have us blame the Vietnam heroin

87

problem on somebody else, possibly the drug pushers (as we do here), the corrupt Saigon government, or a Communist strategy. But the fact that American GIs *wanted* heroin is the problem. We should recognize that heroin has provided servicemen a psychological escape from the feelings of total frustration, hopelessness and boredom associated with winding down a losing battle. Regardless of all the scary stories about heroin, "scag" is probably the only drug that can always make you feel better. And that is why heroin has long been used in our inner cities. The question then becomes, "why is heroin now used in suburbia?"

ASSISTANCE FOR PLANNERS, HEALTH PROFESSIONALS, AND POLICY-MAKERS

The National Association of Social Workers now has a comprehensive policy statement on drug abuse[4] which can be helpful to those working in the field. Based on the functional approach developed by the Mental Health Planning Committee of Milwaukee County, the statement presents the basic concepts and guidelines necessary for problem analysis as well as social policy objectives.

The basic thesis of the policy statement is that "drug abuse" must be defined according to the dysfunctional consequences of drug use. Where no negative consequences exist, drug abuse does not exist. If, however, drug use results in physical, psychological or social dysfunctions then drug abuse exists and should be *treated,* not punished.

Social policy objectives are outlined for the individual and his family, for the local community and for the nation, and all relate to the enhancement of the functioning of the individual in society. Objectives are offered for drug control legislation to control the quantity, availability and advertising of all high abuse potential drugs.

The ramifications of this approach are summarized in a remark by Dr. Daniel X. Friedman:

"While we can define unwanted drug use and differentiate it from unwise or unhealthy drug use, the issue is always that of human behavior. While we can readily define appropriate and inappropriate behavior according to our needs, it seems imperative that we go to the

---

[4] "Policy Statement on Drug Abuse," National Association of Social Workers, 2 Park Avenue, New York, New York 10016.

trouble and confusion of sorting out the issues of drugs, persons, occasions, desired and undesired outcomes, and appropriate social responses." [5]

Drug education is widely recognized as a necessary part of the fight against drug abuse, but there is a curious paradox involved, especially in programs for adults one usually finds himself up against well-entrenched attitudes based upon misinformation and stereotypes. Consequently, we spend much time in dealing with these attitudes, only to read in the paper the following day statements by politicians or public officials which perpetuate the attitudes we try to change. It is ridiculous to spend large amounts of tax money to change the attitudes of the public only to have our efforts undermined. As professionals we must direct a large part of our educational efforts at decision-makers who are responsible for setting the framework and climate of opinion within which we all must function.

ASSISTANCE FOR PARENTS
Considering our drug-oriented culture, our changing social norms, the experimental nature of youth and the availability of mood-altering drugs, it is important for families to be prepared to deal with a drug situation when it arises. The following guidelines have been developed by the Department of Youth Development of the University of Wisconsin Extension.

If you learn that your son or daughter has used drugs, stay calm. Experimentation is part of the growth process, and drug experimentation does not necessarily mean that a youth has an emotional problem, although some young people who decide to use drugs will experience significant personal problems caused by or related to them. Adolescence is at best a difficult time; it can be punctuated by unwanted pregnancies, running away, drug use. Each situation must be handled with the care and concern that should exemplify the parent-child relationship.

If your son or daughter becomes seriously involved in drugs, seek outside help. A mental health center, social service agency or a drug

---

[5] Daniel X. Friedman, M.D., "What Is Drug Abuse?" Paper presented at the Drug Abuse in Industry Symposium, Philadelphia, Pa., May 18, 1970. Quoted in "A Functional Approach to the Problem of Drug Abuse: Phase I of a Community Plan for Drug Abuse Treatment and Prevention," Mental Health Planning Committee of Milwaukee County.

clinic may be helpful, as would consultation with psychiatrists, psychologists, physicians, social workers or clergymen who have relevant experience. Keep in mind that the drug experience has likely filled a gap or has helped the young person cope with life. Positive alternatives to "turning on" are probably the best solution to the problem.

The unreliable quality of drugs obtained illegally, the effects of "good" drugs on certain individuals, and the circumstances surrounding the drug experience itself may result in dangerous or frightening reactions. These sometimes need medical management; they always require understanding, compassion and patience instead of moralizing and panic. A person on a bad trip may feel he is going crazy or dying. He needs to be reassured that the feeling is the effect of a drug in his system, and that it will wear off.

Educate yourself about drugs. Share what you learn with your children, and listen to what they have to say. Don't avoid the issue, but stay away from preaching. Try not to barricade yourself behind the point of view that you as an adult feel obliged to take.

Set good examples. If your concern is really about drug abuse instead of the life-style and behaviors commonly associated with drugs, you must examine your own drug usage in order to be credible. Drugs found in the home are dangerous too, although legal. Diet pills (amphetamines), sleeping tablets (barbiturates), and tranquilizers are common. Hypocritical attitudes about these and about tobacco and alcohol will decrease the likelihood that your children will learn to enjoy life without the help of mind-altering substances. And if you rely on any of the "household drugs," arguing that "I need them but I know how to use them," you really have no retort—honestly, objectively or scientifically—when your youngster counters with "Pot is just as safe, and I know how to use it."

Share your feelings with your children. Adolescent drug users often express unsatisfied needs for close and intimate relationships. Young people today are deeply concerned about communication, caring, and dealing with feelings.

ASSISTANCE FOR SCHOOLS

The goal of our schools must be to help youth develop successful human relationships and personal strength. Rather than one-shot special assemblies and crisis programs, it has been found far more successful to sponsor small-group discussions with competent leaders. Good drug education does not consist simply of pamphlets and films. Exaggeration and sensationalism have no place in the school. School drug policies which view drugs only as a legal problem will foster fear, disrespect and alienation.

Teachers and counselors ought to learn about drugs and why they are used. State and national organizations can offer valuable assistance. (Some of these are listed further on.) It is important for teachers and counselors to examine their own attitudes to determine whether they are qualified to be helpful to young people in the area of drugs.

WHAT CAN THE COMMUNITY DO?

Of course there can be no set program for communities, varying as they do in size, makeup, degree of drug problem, if any. However, it's safe to say that community efforts everywhere must face the most critical aspects of that problem first. Priorities must be based on a thorough understanding of the local situation.

Communities where significant drug abuse exists must provide services to alleviate the present problem and attack the causes. Hospital emergency rooms should be prepared to handle drug reactions and bad trips appropriately. Twenty-four-hour emergency services should be available. Group living experiences such as Synanon may be required. Mental-health centers should have staff trained in helping the drug user and his family. It is essential that the individual be able to approach these services without fear of prosecution. Drug abuse is a *health problem* which we have called "illegal." Resources must be geared to deal with that dilemma.

Where there is traffic in narcotics and other dangerous drugs, there is a great likelihood that arrests are of users, not purveyors. The real culprit is protected by a network of organized crime. Rarely are any of these criminals apprehended, removed as they are from the actual sale by a chain of distributors, and shielded by their stranglehold on officials in too many cities. A community can, at a minimum, *limit* narcotics traffic if its members are collectively determined and demand action.

WHAT CAN WE ALL DO?

Newspapers, television and periodicals have brought the drug problem into every home in the country. On one page a liquor advertisement asks, "What do you drink when you grow up?" (Arrow cordials), while another carries a warning to our children of the dangers of drug abuse. An insensitive communications media, ill informed and unadvised, can only complicate matters. In some instances drug abuse is kept an issue by nothing more than political rhetoric passed on dutifully by the media. Some of the media's attention to the drug issue is helpful, and some is based on the sensationalism that sells air time.

In states where drug users and user-sellers are being imprisoned without access to treatment services, legislative steps must be taken to provide viable alternatives for the courts. Correctional institutions should be searched for persons whose only offense was *possession* of a dangerous drug so that these cases can be reevaluated.

In your state and nationally you should support—with letter writing, telephone calls, telegrams—programs and legislation which will enable drug problems to be *treated,* not *punished.* In Wisconsin new and progressive laws have been enacted so that a user of marijuana can receive a probationary sentence. If it is successfully completed, the record may be wiped clean. Legislation has been introduced to make treatment and rehabilitation an alternative.

Your support is also required for federal legislation designed to prevent trafficking in dangerous drugs. Measures should be aimed at organized crime and narcotics traffic, and at the regulation of the "legitimate" drug industry and its channels of distribution. Regulation of drug traffic must be accomplished without sacrificing individual liberties guaranteed under the Constitution.

We do have a serious drug problem in this country. Strip away the sensationalism, the damaging do-gooders, the make-hay politicians, the crime syndicate; *the problem is still there.* Perhaps, next to the drug purveyors, *we* are the basic cause. We are innocent in the sense that we have been bred with established attitudes. We are guilty when we refuse to discard them to be replaced with learning. If we learn, we may be able to move our society toward one where heavy use of drugs is not only undesirable, but unnecessary. If we don't, I have a prediction. If the causes of drug abuse—in the ghetto and out of it—are related to despair, frustration and hopelessness, then it is doubly disheartening to note that a recent study[6] in New

---

[6] See Herbert Hendin, *Black Suicide* (New York: Basic Books, 1969; New York: Harper & Row, 1971).

York City showed the suicide rate for Blacks, aged 20-35, to be twice that of Whites of the same age.

These deaths are tragic in themselves, but their implication is equally so: when the romance of drugs wears off and the hard, cold realities of life remain, suicide—the ultimate escape—may logically follow drug abuse. If that happens, will America sigh, blame it on something or other, and warn its children of the dangers of "life abuse"?

CHAPTER 7

THE CRUTCH THAT CRIPPLES

THE CRUTCH THAT CRIPPLES[1]

BY AMERICAN MEDICAL ASSOCIATION

Some individuals feel compelled to abuse drugs as a way of life—a way to shut out the real world or enter a world of unreality.

Others, especially young people, may see drug abuse as an adventure—a road to supposedly new experiences.

For all of us, drug abuse is an expensive practice. Millions of tax dollars are spent each year controlling abuse and treating persons dependent on drugs. Equally important, additional millions are lost by those who, often unknowingly, rob themselves of their ability to be productive, and jeopardize their physical and mental health.

The pressures of modern society contribute to the drug-abuse problem. So do its material advantages. Among those youngsters and others who do not have to struggle for the essentials of life, some may turn to drugs for excitement. It seems they have learned how to use their minds, but not how to develop and enjoy their senses without artificial stimulation.

Most of us take drugs for medical reasons. People with headaches or colds take aspirin. Heart patients take digitalis. People with peptic ulcers take antacids.

Drugs are chemicals that act upon the body's own chemistry. Sometimes they substitute for chemicals the body may lack, such as insulin. Frequently they help fight infections or improve our ability to function by stepping up or slowing down the activity of our glands and organs.

It is clear that drugs can promote and preserve good health when

---

[1] Report of Committee on Alcoholism and Drug Dependence, Council on Mental Health, American Medical Association, 1968. Used by permission.

they are taken on the advice of a physician, or according to directions on the label.

On the other hand, drug abuse—taking drugs without professional advice or direction—can injure vital parts of the body: the liver, the kidneys, the heart, the brain. Abuse of certain drugs also can lead to drug dependence, either psychological, physical, or both.

Drug dependence, although seldom fatal, can cripple its victims in body and mind—in some cases, permanently.

What is drug dependence?

Which drugs can cause dependence?

What are proper uses for these drugs in medical treatment?

Why do people abuse drugs?

What effects do abusers experience, and what are some of the results of their dependence?

Can drug abuse be prevented?

This article is an attempt to answer these questions. It was written not only because drugs are being abused by millions in the United States today, but because drug dependence goes far beyond the individuals directly involved. It touches the life of everyone.

Drug dependence comes about from taking certain drugs regularly and often in increasing amounts and at shorter intervals.

Dependence is based on a psychological or emotional need to continue taking a drug because of the relief of uncomfortable tension or the apparent feelings of pleasure or well-being that can result. In the case of drugs that depress the central nervous system, dependence also is based on a physical need, added to the psychological.

Abuse of narcotics, for example, causes both physical and psychological dependence. Abuse of LSD or marijuana can cause only psychological dependence, harmful in itself.

Drug abuse does not always result in dependence. When it does, it is because the roots of dependence lie within the psychological makeup of the individual himself, rather than in the properties of the drug. The drug feeds these roots and makes them grow. If the individual had not turned to drugs for this "nourishment" he might have used other harmful means of relieving his tensions and anxieties. Or, with help, he could have found constructive ways to deal with his problems.

Many drugs can lead to dependence through abuse. Those most

often abused fall into four major categories: (1) the narcotics (pain-killers), such as heroin, codeine, and morphine, (2) the sedatives, such as barbiturates, tranquilizers, and alcohol, (3) the stimulants, such as the amphetamines, and (4) the hallucinogens, such as LSD and marijuana.

MEDICAL USES OF
THESE DRUGS

Most of the narcotics, barbiturates, and amphetamines have a proper place in the legitimate medical treatment of physical and mental illness. This is not true of the hallucinogens.

Narcotics, which come from the opium poppy, are administered by physicians to relieve pain. When a patient has acute pain, the physician tries to get at the cause and eliminate it quickly. Sometimes when that isn't possible, or as a part of treatment, he will prescribe morphine or a similar pain-killer. When he does, the patient gets the drug only when significant pain returns. The less the drug has to be used, the better.

There is good reason for this. It seems that certain central-nervous-system cells actually become dependent on the narcotic's presence by adjusting their activity to the drug. When this happens the cells, in effect, hunger for more, and, if they don't get it, withdrawal symptoms appear.

Paregoric and codeine are other narcotic drugs used in medicine. Paregoric is prescribed for intestinal trouble, and codeine is a common ingredient in cough syrup and pain-killers. Taken as directed, they don't present problems.

Barbiturates are sedatives which also play an important part in medical practice. Either singly, or as the principal ingredients in mixtures, they can be effective in treating epilepsy, insomnia, and emotional and mental illness. Significant quantities beyond proper use usually are necessary to cause physical dependence.

Amphetamines and other stimulants, popularly known as pep pills, are prescribed for certain types of mild depression and as short-term aids in weight control. Stimulants do not cause physical dependence, even when abused. But because psychological dependence and side effects can occur rapidly, the physician prescribes these drugs for only a limited time and for a specific purpose.

WHO ARE
THE DRUG ABUSERS?

Patients who take drugs under a physician's orders can abuse them, intentionally or otherwise, by not following directions.

The majority of abusers, however, are persons who do not take drugs under medical supervision.

There is the unemployed young man with no prospects of a job who shoots heroin into his arm to forget his problems; the housewife who takes tranquilizers, or drinks regularly, to dull the constant noise of her bickering children; the truck driver who swallows pep pills to keep awake on an all-night run; the college sophomore who turns his back on society with disgust and uses LSD to take a trip away from the real world and to a "society" of his own making.

People of all ages, from all walks of life, and in all economic and social circumstances, abuse drugs. Each of the four categories of the dependence-producing drugs tends to have its own type of abusers and its own physical and emotional consequences.

Heroin, or "smack" as it is often called, would not be available if the laws were obeyed. In this country, as in most others, it cannot be made, sold, or used legally. But it is manufactured and smuggled in from other countries in quantities sufficient to maintain more than 60,000 persons in a state of dependence.

Most of these dependent persons live in or around large cities, and the majority are men. They usually are young—under thirty. Some don't live long because they run themselves down physically; others "mature out" of their dependence. One study of 7,200 former addicts showed the majority of them voluntarily stopped using heroin by age thirty-five; by age forty-seven, all but 13 percent had done so.

Typically, heroin abusers have financial problems, particularly because of their habit. Well over half of them are Negroes and Puerto Ricans, and as such they also may have social problems. But it is apparent that other factors are involved. Most persons in similar circumstances and with the same cultural backgrounds don't abuse narcotics.

As in the case of most drug-dependent persons, heroin abusers tend to have dependent personalities to start with. Often they have a history of being treated like children even past adolescence by over-protective mothers. They feel insecure and inferior, and they try to counteract these feelings with drugs. Usually they will experiment with drugs other than heroin first, notably marijuana, and find that

100

these drugs don't blot out their emotional pain. It is also common for heroin abusers to continue taking other drugs along with heroin.

The old picture of the "dope fiend" who rapes and murders is not an accurate one. Heroin abusers seldom commit crimes of violence, and they have little interest in sex as such. Many do have a history of delinquent behavior before they became addicts, and often after they are addicted they will steal to get money to maintain their habit. Thus, a large proportion of the crime in New York City has been traced to addicts. Their offenses consist mainly of burglary, shoplifting, prostitution.

Heroin can be so addicting, both physically and psychologically, that once a person is "hooked" he thinks of little else. For him, heroin becomes a way of life. His main concern in the morning is to get his wake-up fix. He will dissolve some heroin powder on a spoon, draw it into a hypodermic syringe or dropper through a piece of cotton which acts as a filter, and then inject it into a vein. He will repeat this process one or more times during the day. Generally, the *longer* he takes the drug the *more* he will take because his body needs increasing amounts. His last business before the end of the day is to make sure he has a supply for the next morning.

Getting a person to give up his habit is not easy. Addicts may come in voluntarily for treatment when they realize they have little hope of raising themselves out of their dismal condition. Some states have compulsory commitment—addicts are sent to hospitals rather than jails when they are arrested for possession of the drug. Under federal law, persons who are addicts and are charged with, or convicted of, a federal offense, can be committed for treatment. Addicts not charged with any offense also may be committed if they seek help.

Withdrawal from heroin need not be dangerous or even very painful. Many addicts are able to withdraw without help. Symptoms begin about eight hours after abstinence in the average case and reach a peak in about forty hours. Starting with a running nose, tearing eyes, perspiration, and goose flesh, the addict later experiences cramps, muscle twitching, vomiting, diarrhea, and insomnia in varying degrees.

Though highly discomforting, withdrawal is not the hardest part of the treatment process. More difficult is keeping the addict from backsliding once withdrawal is completed—overcoming his underlying psychological need to take the drug. Hospitals, physicians, and social service organizations all try to rehabilitate the heroin abuser to make it possible for him to take his place in society in a drug-free condition.

With or without treatment, an addict may "mature out" of his dependence on drugs. But the odds are long against immediate success. The roots of insecurity and immaturity, which led him to drugs in the first place, go deep. If he returns to the same surroundings he left, he may well experience the old frustrations and temptations with "assistance" from his associates and the pushers.

Nevertheless, every heroin-dependent person should be encouraged to seek help. Although the road to recovery is rough and often seemingly endless, treatment is still his best hope.

ABUSE OF SEDATIVES

Until the middle of the nineteenth century, those looking for substances to ease their tensions had to depend almost entirely on herbs and alcoholic beverages. In the 1850's, however, new chemical compounds known as bromides were introduced and immediately became popular as sedatives. And with use came abuse.

Abuse of bromides waned in the 1930's, when other more powerful sedatives called barbiturates were introduced. Especially subject to abuse are the short-acting ones like pentobarbital, secobarbital, and amobarbital. Phenobarbital and other long-acting barbiturates are not frequently abused because they don't produce quick effects. Since the 1950's, the tranquilizers, another class of sedative-type drugs, have been abused in much the same manner as the short-acting barbiturates.

Because barbiturate prescriptions must be ordered by physicians, and dispensing by drugstores is controlled by law, the huge quantities sufficient to maintain abuse come largely through illegal channels. The person who becomes dependent on barbiturates may first have used the drug under a doctor's care. But others simply learn something of the drug's intoxicating effects and begin to experiment and self-prescribe.

Many of those abusing barbiturates might be called "silent abusers." They take pills in the privacy of their homes and do not cause disturbances in their community. These are mainly middle-aged and older persons—the types not often found abusing other kinds of drugs.

Most abusers of barbiturates who become dependent are individuals who find life's tensions and anxieties unbearable. Like alcoholics, they need the feeling of security and well-being they believe their drug will give them. Indeed it may give it to them while they are "drunk." But, as in alcoholic intoxication, there can be other effects: confusion, irritability, incoordination, and depression. Even when the effects are desirable, the person is later faced with his same old tensions and anxieties, plus a hangover.

That is why some carry their abuse to such an extreme that they remain bed-ridden in a constant state of semi-stupor. Suicide can occur through overdose, intentional or otherwise. With narcotics, suicide from overdose is rare because increasing tolerance raises the lethal limit. This limit is not raised significantly by barbiturate tolerance.

A few persons abuse barbiturates for reasons other than release from tension and anxiety.

There are those who take them in combination with another drug to get "far-out" results. When the other drug is alcohol or one of the narcotics, a possible far-out result is death, because each drug increases the action of the other. When the other drug is a pep pill, the abuser gets on a seesaw of sedation and stimulation.

In some unusual cases, barbiturates are taken for exhilaration and for a sense of increased efficiency, just like pep pills. This may happen after tolerance develops through prolonged abuse, because the drug can have a stimulating rather than a depressing effect.

Barbiturates also are used as a temporary substitute for narcotics when addicts run out of heroin.

The long-term abuse of barbiturates causes strong physical dependence, making withdrawal a serious business. Withdrawal from narcotics is bad enough, but barbiturate withdrawal, if abrupt and sudden, can be fatal.

Physicians know that the process must be accomplished very slowly and carefully. Preferably the patient should be in a hospital, where he can be observed constantly. Short of death, withdrawal complications can include convulsions and delirium.

ABUSE OF STIMULANTS

Although amphetamines and related stimulants are, like the barbiturates, legally available only by prescription, supplies move briskly through the black market.

Some persons abuse these drugs to overcome depression or to

combat fatigue. More numerous are those who take them not to attain feelings of well-being, but to go beyond to exhilaration and super-sensitivity. Generally these are younger people who experiment with a variety of drugs and who may abuse a combination of them.

Recently, they have taken to injecting amphetamine to get faster and more intense results. Some claim they can achieve a kind of "controlled hypersensitivity" from a combination of amphetamine, barbiturate, and heroin.

When large doses of amphetamine are taken, either orally or by injection, tolerance can build up quickly, and then larger and larger doses become necessary to attain the desired effects. One of the chief hazards of abusing stimulants is that a person can overestimate his physical capabilities. These drugs mask underlying fatigue caused by unusual expenditure of energy and lack of rest. That is why after an amphetamine spree, a person may collapse from exhaustion. He can also suffer damage to his circulatory system.

Another possible complication is a mental illness known as amphetamine psychosis in some individuals who take sizable doses for a long time. In this condition, the patient believes others are plotting to harm him and he has hallucinations—seeing or hearing things that aren't there.

Fortunately, withdrawal from amphetamines is usually painless—physically. Psychologically, abrupt withdrawal can bring on serious depression with potential suicide. And because stimulants frequently are abused in combination with other drugs, the effects of withdrawal from the others also must be taken into account. For these reasons, it is best that withdrawal be carried out in a hospital under a physician's supervision.

Hallucinogens are unique among the drugs that can cause dependence because they have no accepted use in medical practice.

Strictly speaking, a hallucinogen is a drug that produces hallucinations. Actually, there are fewer hallucinations than distortions—seeing or hearing things in a different way than they actually are.

Many substances have properties which can cause distortions, including morning-glory seeds and an extract from a Mexican mushroom called psilocybin. First in popularity among the hallucinogens is marijuana. Next, and by far the most potent and dangerous of all, is LSD.

ACCIDENTAL DISCOVERY

LSD is an abbreviation for *lysergic acid diethylamide,* a chemical so powerful that an amount smaller than a grain of salt can cause intoxication.

Its effects were discovered in 1943 by a chemist who had made it in a Swiss pharmaceutical laboratory five years earlier. He accidentally swallowed a bit of it and soon entered a weird realm of odd-shaped undulating objects of vivid color.

After he reported his experience, some scientists thought LSD might be useful in studying schizophrenia—a mental disorder in which patients live all or part of their lives in fantasy. Carefully controlled research into its possible medical uses was begun and still goes on.

Meanwhile, the word was out. Some fairly prominent persons, among them authors, movie stars, and university instructors, experimented with LSD and gave to the public glowing accounts of their "trips." Two educators became convinced that LSD could expand the mind and allow people to make use of talents and abilities they didn't know they had. They started an LSD crusade, directed particularly at college students and other young adults.

Since then, abuse has spread rapidly throughout this and other countries. Studies of those who have taken the drug are now revealing why they take it, what they get out of it, and what happens to them later. It is not the bright picture painted at first.

PURPOSEFUL PURSUIT

Like other drugs, LSD is tried by many who are simply curiosity seekers. For the most part, however, abuse has been purposeful especially among young people. They are looking either for pleasure or self-improvement.

The pleasure-seekers are generally a passive lot. They sit fascinated while new sounds, shapes, colors, and smells flood their senses, and new thoughts about themselves and their relationships to others intrigue their minds.

The self-improvers are more serious. They too experience these effects, but they try to act upon them. They are not like the pleasure-seekers who have, as one abuser put it, "a whole new team of horses without a wagon to hitch them to."

For the painter, the poet, the musician, LSD may mistakenly appear to be a vehicle for creating more original and more meaningful works of art. Although several creative persons have claimed success, objective observers recognize few if any improvements.

One observer has stressed the fantasy nature of these claims. Many who talk about writing great novels or poetry never seem to get around to it—the most notable thing about their "heightened creative powers" is inaction, he says.

Another, commenting on the same phenomenon, declared that "a good writer or poet works hard, and drugs prevent hard work. Maturity is gained by recognizing one's own limits of creativity, and drugs may only provide an illusion that one is a good artist."

THE DISENCHANTED

There is another type of serious abuser. He is not like the typical narcotics addict who personally may know the pangs of poverty or prejudice. He is usually well-fed, well-clothed, and well-regarded. But he sees that poverty and prejudice do exist in some places, he sees nations at war, he sees automation taking over, he sees adults setting one standard for youth and another for themselves.

To him, trying to right wrongs is a waste of time. He believes society is incurably sick, and he wants no part of it. The wagon he takes on his "trip" leads to a society of his own filled with sensory delights and revelations of the meaning of life, love, and brotherhood. He may seek out others of similar bent so together they can form back-to-nature colonies, grow their own food, and enter the old world only to get money to buy marijuana and LSD.

From this vantage point, he sees society no longer as ugly, but ridiculous. He looks down and watches people playing games—the husband-wife game, the teacher-pupil school game, the nine-to-five office game, the cold-war game.

LSD itself does not create such attitudes. Other young people not on drugs also may see society as a series of farces. But LSD does facilitate these attitudes by loosening the abuser's hold on reality.

It appears that LSD may have a specific toxic effect on the retina of the eye, the optic pathways, or the visual cortex. After taking LSD, a person will go through an average of eight hours of watching familiar objects take on new forms, feeling that he is outside himself looking in, hearing new sounds from an old phonograph record, or seeing colors he never saw before.

The trip is not always pleasant. It can be harrowing. The distorted objects and sounds, the illusory colors, the new thoughts—all may be menacing and terrifying. A trip like that usually eliminates the pleasure-seeker. It may not deter others.

ECHOES FROM HOSPITALS

No one, not even a trained psychiatrist, can say for sure whether a person will have complications if he takes LSD. The fact is there is no basis for identifying those for whom any drug is safe. Even for the same individual, effects can vary from one time to the next.

Drug experimenters often think: "It won't hurt to try it, just once." With LSD, "just once" can be once too often.

Cases have been reported of recurring LSD intoxication over a period of months even though the person did not take more than one dose. It also is evident now that just a single dose can trigger mental illness. In a study at a New York hospital of 52 patients with LSD-induced psychosis, it was found that 26 had taken the drug only once.

Hospitals are seeing more and more of such cases. Some of these patients had previous mental or emotional disorders, but others were apparently normal before their trips. Only 12 of the New York patients showed evidence of underlying psychosis.

On the other hand, an analysis of the history of 20 patients in a San Francisco hospital revealed that in 75 percent of the cases, LSD was not the major factor leading to hospitalization. Usually, there was a series of attempts to cope with emotional problems, including the abuse of several drugs.

Although it is too early to tell, there is a possibility that LSD can cause permanent brain damage and can injure hereditary genes. One experiment has implicated LSD in damage to the chromosomes resulting in white-blood-cell abnormalities. Eight users of LSD and nine nonusers were studied. In six of the LSD group, chromosomal breakage was found to be about three times greater than the expected or normal rate. Only one nonuser had significant breakage, and he had received a series of x-ray treatments several years earlier.

FORWARD FROM POT

Marijuana probably is abused by youth more than any other drug. It comes from the flowering tops of the hemp plant which are dried, powdered, and rolled into cigarettes called reefers.

Smoking marijuana, or pot, produces feelings of well-being and also sensory distortions. These effects, though similar in kind to those produced by LSD and other potent hallucinogens, are far less intense. Ironically, this is marijuana's chief danger, because the user may then try stronger substances, including heroin.

Although marijuana does not lead inevitably to heroin abuse, it is a fact that most heroin abusers have experimented first with marijuana. Traditionally, they have been introduced to both drugs through friends or other contacts in the "hard drug" culture.

But the problem now is a much broader one. Pot parties are common among certain groups of college and high school students. For them, smoking marijuana has become an "in" thing to do. It carries with it the excitement of doing something illegal and the satisfaction of rebelling against authority.

Fortunately, most youngsters who try pot give it up after the novelty wears off and they realize that the kicks they get aren't worth the risks.

A sizable minority, however, are discontented with what they experience. They expect ever-increasing pleasurable effects, and they don't get them. Some will turn to heroin, but more of the discontented will try other drugs, particularly LSD, because they don't want to risk physical dependence. They often will continue on pot while taking other drugs in sequence or at the same time.

Although there is no evidence that marijuana causes any lasting physical or mental changes, recent studies indicate that hashish, a stronger cousin of marijuana prevalent in Africa and the Middle East, may do so. Hashish also can be obtained in this country. When a teenager is handed a reefer, he can't be sure it's just marijuana. It may be hashish, or a mixture containing hashish or even other more potent hallucinogens.

Proponents of marijuana claim the drug is less harmful than alcohol and that therefore it should be legalized. They overlook, or choose to ignore, important differences.

First, most persons usually do not take alcohol to the point of intoxication. One or two drinks a day normally have little effect. On the other hand, one or two reefers can produce marijuana intoxication.

Second, alcohol, even when it is abused, is compatible with a considerable period of productivity. The action of marijuana is far more rapid. It quickly interferes with social and economic productivity.

Finally, many drunks are aware that they can't handle certain tasks, such as driving, and they don't attempt them. But marijuana smokers as a rule have a false sense of ability, and the consequences can be serious.

Thus, both during and after intoxication, the abuser can misjudge distances and miscalculate time. Stepping off a curb into the street can be a major project. Crossing the street, or operating a car, can be a disaster.

Marijuana abusers often are listless, neglect their personal appearance, and feel they are failures after they see that they can't accomplish the great things they thought they could while under the influence of the drug. Continuous abuse also may intensify temporary psychiatric illness.

For many, however, marijuana is most harmful as the teacher of "Drug Abuse A-1," an introductory course in the pleasures and pitfalls of dependence—where the pleasures seem to promise more to come and the pitfalls appear minor and easily avoided.

BUMPING INTO REALITY
Whether they like it or not, drug abusers have to live in society. Even LSD colonists can't remain out of touch.

Physical illness or injury, both during and after intoxication, is not uncommon. Nor are mental disorders of varying degrees and kinds.

Returning to a comparatively cold and mundane world after intoxication can be discouraging and depressing—enough to shatter any remaining emotional stability. Three LSD users, all of whom had a history of schizophrenic behavior, believed they had achieved new personalities by taking the drug. When the effects wore off, however, they discovered that their friends didn't recognize their so-called "new image." Instead of accepting the fact, they refused to give up their altered conception of themselves. They had to be hospitalized —one was paranoid and the other two were catatonic, unable to assert themselves in any way.

Those who are drug dependent may neglect their personal habits or appearance, even to the detriment of their health. They go without food, inviting malnutrition. The mainliners, those who inject heroin or other drugs into their veins, risk blood poisoning, tetanus, hepatitis, and other serious infections caused by unclean equipment.

Then there are the accidents. One LSD abuser walked out of a window several stories up because he believed he could fly. Another became a statistic when he thought he could stop traffic by standing on an expressway with his hand raised. Other accidents, many fatal, are caused by people driving under the distorting influence of drugs.

Everyone would like to turn on contentment and turn off discomfort at will. Drug abusers think they can. The trouble is that the facts of life, human and otherwise, cannot be changed with an injection or a swallow.

WHERE TO GET HELP

Although society doesn't permit people who are drug dependent to have their own way, it does try to help them overcome their habit.

Many want help and seek it out, others have to be persuaded.

It is not easy for the average person to recognize someone who is abusing drugs. Symptoms are varied, sometimes vague, and often similar to those of other conditions. Drug abuse may be suspected, however, if the following signs are present.

1. Inability to coordinate when standing or walking, muddled speech, and impaired judgment can indicate barbiturate abuse. This intoxication closely resembles drunken behavior, except the individual doesn't smell of alcohol.

2. Rapid pulse, restlessness, jittery muscular twitches, heavy sweating, and bad breath are hallmarks of amphetamine abuse. The individual also tends to be nervous, highly talkative, and overactive.

3. Marijuana abuse typically leads to increased appetite with an especial craving for sweets. As mentioned before, the user is often apathetic, listless, and careless about his personal habits.

4. If a person has widely dilated pupils and constantly wears dark glasses, even at night, LSD or marijuana may be involved.

5. Pin-point pupils, on the other hand, are a sign of possible abuse of heroin or another narcotic drug. So are chills and needle marks on the arms and legs. Addicts often wear long-sleeve sweaters or jackets, even in summer, both to keep warm and to hide their scars.

Another way to tell if a person is taking drugs is to listen to the language he uses. The jargon of drug abusers has spilled over, to a certain extent, to the speech of the younger generation. "Turn on," "kicks," and similar expressions, once the property of the abuser world, are now in common usage. Certain words and phrases, however, are exclusively in the abuser's vernacular.

"Mainlining," for example, means injecting a drug into the veins.

"Pot head" and "acid head" refer respectively to abusers of marijuana and LSD.

"Barbs," "goofballs," and "candy" are popular slang for barbiturates.

Amphetamine abusers may refer to their drugs as "bennies," "co-pilots," or "wake-ups."

If you do know someone who is dependent on drugs, the best thing you can do is get medical attention for him.

If you don't know a physician, call the county medical society or one of your local hospitals. They can give you the information you need.

Proper medical care is an essential first step. The physician will know whether to administer another drug to counteract the effects of the drug being abused. He will know how to treat other illness brought about by drug abuse. He will arrange for hospitalization if necessary.

He also will undertake the next step, often in consultation with a psychiatrist or with counseling services in the community. That step is the treatment of the mental and emotional disorders which preceded or resulted from drug dependence. As in all illness, the chances for recovery are better the earlier treatment is started.

THE PREVENTION OF ABUSE

Laws against drug abuse have been enacted to protect people from harming themselves and society.

Most drugs which have use in medical practice can be obtained legally only by prescription if they have a potential for causing dependence.

Physicians and others dealing with narcotic drugs for medical purposes are required to register, pay special taxes, and keep accurate records of how the drugs are dispensed.

Certain narcotics, such as paregoric, and preparations like cough syrups which contain narcotics, are considered exempt and in many states may be obtained without a prescription. The pharmacist, however, is required to keep a complete record of who buys these preparations.

The penalties, under federal laws, for the illegal sale or transfer of narcotics and marijuana are stiff: for the first offense, 5 to 20 years; for succeeding offenses, 10 to 40 years. In addition, fines of up to

$20,000 may be levied. Illegal possession can incur penalties of from 2 to 10 years for the first offense, 5 to 20 years for the second, and 10 to 40 years for additional offenses.

Most states have laws modeled after the federal acts.

Certain stimulants, depressants, and hallucinogens are controlled under the Drug Abuse Control Amendments to the Federal Food, Drug, and Cosmetic Act.

For those dangerous drugs used in medical practice, special conditions must be met by manufacturers, and distributors, including product purity and the keeping of accurate records of receipts and sales. Prescriptions older than six months cannot be filled, and refills are limited.

Only one company is licensed to produce LSD and then only for research purposes. Most other hallucinogens cannot be made or sold legally.

Illegal production and sale of dangerous drugs also can result in fines and imprisonment, although not as severe as under the narcotics laws.

State laws covering these drugs are varied.

There is no question that laws serve as a deterrent. But despite the penalties involved, drug abuse is on the increase. One reason is the tremendous profits that can be made in the black market. Even though enforcement agencies crack down hard on smuggling, enough marijuana and heroin gets through to keep the illicit trade well supplied. The narcotics racketeers also have gone into the pill business, diverting barbiturates and amphetamines for illegal distribution. Some have set up legal fronts and make pills themselves to supply the black market.

It is estimated that of the more than 10 billion amphetamine and barbiturate pills made each year, about half go through illegal channels to abusers.

Because LSD and other hallucinogens have been outlawed since 1966, the quality of these drugs is particularly questionable. Much of the LSD available today is made by individual amateurs who are looking for quick profits, or who take the drug themselves and want others to share their experiences. The inferior nature of this "bathtub acid" increases the possibility of a "bad trip."

If it is difficult to control manufacturing and smuggling, it is even more difficult to police distribution. Pushers of narcotics and pills are clever in their dealings. Because of the tiny dosages required, LSD is particularly hard to detect.

WHAT YOU CAN DO

One thing you can do is make sure you don't get trapped yourself. If you are taking any of these drugs under a doctor's orders, follow his orders to the letter. Don't take more than he tells you to, or take drugs more often than he directs.

Don't share your drugs with another person, even if he seems to have the same illness or condition you have. Tell him to see his doctor and get his own prescription.

As tactfully as you can, try to point out to the drug abuser the dangers, realizing that he probably is convinced he is helping instead of hurting himself. Encourage him to see a physician, because the abuser often needs medical care and treatment.

If you are aware of any illegal traffic in drugs, give accurate information to your police department or to a branch of the Federal Bureau of Narcotics and Dangerous Drugs, if one is located in your community.

If you are a parent, try to develop in your children, from the time they are babies, the fortitude they will need later to face the difficulties we all meet in life.

A child cannot be completely independent. But he can be taught to make decisions for himself—minor ones at first and more important ones as he grows older. Remember that drug dependence is only one facet of general dependence—relying on a variety of crutches and on other people to solve problems.

Most Americans enjoy a relatively high standard of living. While it has its obvious benefits, prosperity can lead to overindulgence. When that happens, some people may grow tired of what they have and become disillusioned if they don't get more. Others expect life to be all pleasure and no pain.

There are children growing up in the midst of plenty who reflect such attitudes. The bored youth with an exaggerated need to indulge himself is a prime prospect for drug abuse.

This makes it important to encourage your child to see beauty and meaning in the world as it is and as it can be, to help him develop his emotional and spiritual resources, as well as his mind. Many adults who resort to drug abuse are emotionally stunted—they substitute drugs for life experiences they never had.

It is natural for young people to experiment with many things, to question, to examine. But if a youngster is capable of making intelligent decisions based on the facts of drug abuse danger, he may well avoid this kind of experimenting. Moreover, if he genuinely appreciates the many valuable attributes of the world around him, he is not likely to think about trading real living for "kicks"—now or in the future.

WHAT CAN YOU DO ABOUT DRUG ABUSE?

CHAPTER 8

WHAT CAN YOU DO ABOUT DRUG ABUSE?

BY ANDREW A. SORENSEN, PH.D.

The prevalence of drug abuse in our society has been widely discussed and documented. But the seemingly contagious manner in which drug abuse has spread has caused millions of Americans to throw up their hands and say, "There's nothing we can do about it. We'll just have to let it run its course."

However, there *is* something you can do about drug abuse! There are *many* things which you can do both to prevent people who are not using now or using moderately from becoming abusers and to provide more adequate treatment for those who are already abusing drugs or addicted to them. Not one of these courses of action, by itself, will solve the problem or disentangle the complicated web of psychological, sociological, and physiological phenomena which conspire to make drug addiction what it is. However, if we continue to be bewildered by the complexity of issues and refrain from action because the problem is so big and we are so small, we are contributing directly to the spread of drug abuse by our failure to act.

Here are just a few kinds of activities you might get involved in:

I. GENERAL TREATMENT AND PREVENTION PROGRAMS

1. If there is a drug treatment program in your community, inquire about serving in some volunteer capacity. Most of these programs can use a wide variety of talents, from answering the telephone to painting walls, from helping to prepare meals to sweeping floors. But if you will only accept a leadership role in that program or if you feel confident that you know why kids use drugs, you might be advised to stay away from such programs. Most of them have a good supply of

leaders and "experts," but a shortage of volunteers to perform some of the less glamorous tasks.

Hundreds of thousands of communities throughout the United States have meetings of Alcoholics Anonymous (A.A.). A large number of these groups welcomes persons who are (or have been) addicted to drugs other than alcohol. And many persons who are labeled alcoholics are often abusing other drugs at the same time. Therefore, surprising as it may seem, your local A.A. group may be a good source for improving your understanding of drug abuse.

Naturally, there are many groups that are concerned almost exclusively with non-alcoholic drug abuse. These groups are of several different types:

a. *Discussion groups.* Ex-addicts have formed organizations such as Narcotics Anonymous, which usually meet on a weekly basis, giving the persons present an opportunity to discuss how they are currently dealing with their addiction. As with A.A., these groups are generally oriented to abstinence from drugs.

A somewhat unusual group of addicts meets regularly in Chicago under the auspices of CHANCE, Inc., a self-help program run by men who are serving and have served time in prison. The Rev. Albert A. Sorensen, founder of CHANCE and senior Protestant chaplain at the Illinois State Penitentiary at Joliet, discovered that many of the participants in group-therapy programs both inside and outside prison felt that their problems as drug addicts were different from those of non-addicts. Therefore, the ex-addicts formed separate groups for therapy meetings; they welcome interested and concerned persons to take part in their group sessions.

b. *Crash pads and storefronts.* Facilities of this sort provide short-range assistance for persons with a wide variety of problems. Although these programs do not provide the kind of medical care often required by persons withdrawing from heroin or barbiturates, they can give valuable help, for example, to those who are "coming down" from hallucinogenic drugs.

c. *Therapeutic communities.* Perhaps the most famous of the therapeutic communities working with drug abuse in this country are those affiliated with Synanon. Other programs utilizing a similar approach are Odyssey House and Daytop Village. These residential communities usually stipulate that the drug abusers who enter their programs must live in the house on a twenty-four hour per day basis until they have completed a probationary period. These programs strictly prohibit the use of alcohol and narcotic drugs, and rely heavily upon group therapy techniques.

Try to find out if there are treatment programs such as the three types described above in your community. If there are, try to visit them.

2. If there is no program in your community with special emphasis for drugs, there should be. Excluding some ascetic religious communities (and not even all of them), I know of no community in this country where there is absolutely no abuse of drugs (including alcohol and tobacco). So, if you do not yet have a program, you and your neighbors might work together to establish one.

A good place to start is with your local clergymen. A recent survey by the Joint Commission on Mental Illness and Health reported that of the adults who sought help for emotional and mental-health problems, more people consulted clergymen than psychiatrists, psychologists, and social workers combined. Thus it may be that your local clergymen have been counseling with drug abusers and their families, and would welcome the prospect of joining with you to set up a treatment and prevention program.

Local mental-health centers also may prove to be valuable resources in establishing or expanding drug-treatment programs. Or your municipal or county government may be moving to establish some type of treatment or education program. In New York State, for example, many counties have established Narcotic Guidance Councils. These councils may offer information on existing programs and guidelines for developing new ones.

II. "HOTLINES" OR REFERRAL AGENCIES

There are very few cities and towns of appreciable size in the United States that have only one agency which is oriented at least in part to working with drug abusers and drug addicts. For example, in the town of 26,000 in which I live, there are no less than five agencies which offer services for people with drug dependency. It is crucial that there be good communication among the staffs of these agencies in order to provide effective programs and minimize duplication of services. In many areas, hotlines or referral agencies have been established to facilitate this kind of communication, and also offer crisis counseling, referral to various treatment facilities, and general information about drugs.

1. If there is a hotline agency in your community, perhaps you

could help in some way. Usually these programs are eager to accept any person for a volunteer position regardless of age, sex, or extent of formal education. Often these programs insist on an orientation period, both to determine your areas of competence and give you training for dealing with the various kinds of crises you might meet.

2. If there is no hotline program in your community, you might be instrumental in establishing one. A friend of mine started such a service merely by placing a message for persons with drug problems above her home telephone number on several bulletin boards in the neighborhood laundromat, the local high school, and the church she belonged to. She was so inundated with calls that in a short time a hotline program grew out of it. There are indeed dangers in the notion that telephone conversations are panaceas for all kinds of ills, but these programs can be of great assistance to many people.

III. IN-PATIENT HOSPITAL SERVICES

1. Although you may find this surprising, very few hospitals have in-patient treatment facilities for drug abusers and addicts. Learn where the nearest hospital services are. It is quite likely that such a hospital also has an office for volunteer services. Identify yourself to that office, and express your interest in helping with the drug-treatment program. If you do not have the kinds of skills that they require, ask if they have a training program or can recommend one to you. (See section VII below.)

2. If your local hospital does not have in-patient facilities, discuss the need for these facilities with your physician. But don't let matters stop there! Work with both physicians and non-physicians to put pressure on the hospital's board of directors to provide in-patient and medical back-up services for drug abusers. As a dramatic but simple way of assessing the adequacy of your local hospital to provide these kinds of services, ask some staff members this question: If a teenager in your neighborhood takes an overdose of heroin, can he be treated adequately for both overdose and withdrawal?

IV. OUT-PATIENT CLINIC SERVICES

1. Your community may be one of hundreds across the country which has out-patient facilities for drug-dependent persons. These range from "rap" centers (places where people may come to talk with someone) to pharmacologically oriented programs, such as methadone maintenance clinics (where people may receive medica-

tion under medical supervision). Many of these clinics rely heavily upon the help of volunteers. The type of help you can offer may range from listening carefully to someone talk about his problems to assisting in planning a rock concert to raise funds for the program.

2. If your community does not have an out-patient clinic, you may wish to collaborate with others to get one established. The procedure for involvement requires a combination of the suggestions in sections I (item 2) and III (item 2) above. It is crucial to the development of such a clinic whether it is planned to be done *through* your local hospital or *outside* of it. There are no hard and fast rules to govern your decision. I worked in one community where the hospital staff were highly resistant to working with "those crazy drug freaks." It is obvious that if the staff of this particular hospital were pressured into opening an out-patient drug clinic the staff attitudes would militate against the success of the clinic. In that case, it would be much more sensible to develop such a clinic outside the hospital structure. In other communities, the hospital staff will be highly receptive to the request for establishing an out-patient clinic. However, community support for the clinic should be developed before the hospital board is approached. Again, local clergymen can be very helpful in establishing the clinic.

V. SCHOOL DRUG EDUCATION PROGRAMS

Very few of us question the premise that drug education should occur in the schools. Thus we tend to feel that if our schools have a drug-education program "something is being done about drugs in our community." And many promoters of drug-education programs contribute to this set of beliefs by arguing that the earlier we establish a drug-education program in the educational sequence for our country's children, the better off we are.

These arguments are based on several assumptions that need to be examined more carefully. Many of the educational programs sponsored by our school systems are notoriously ineffective. At least part of the massive "drop-out" phenomenon we are witnessing is due to the feeling that what is taught in our schools is not accurate or meaningful (or sensitively communicated). Thus we must not assume that drug-education programs in schools are automatically good. For example, I was in a high-school classroom recently while a teacher who seemed to have little information about drugs other than that contained on the printed pages before him struggled valiantly to "teach" the students about drug abuse. About one-fourth of the way through the class period he passed out a brochure describing the dangers of smoking marijuana. The second statement on the hand-out read: "Smoking marijuana leads to heroin addiction." Many studies have demonstrated that this is not necessarily true. The more sophisticated students were aware of some of these studies, and thus ridiculed the teacher and "turned off" to the rest of what he had to say, although most of what he said later was accurate. Judging from the remarks of several students in the classroom and in a discussion I had with them after the class, I would argue that *no* formal program in drug education would have been better than the one they were exposed to.

Another fallacy which underlies many of our school drug-education programs is that if one demonstrates (preferably visually) the awful consequences of drug abuse, young people will never want to use drugs. Therefore, many educational programs show detailed photographs of "works" (the apparatus used for injecting heroin), people "shooting up," and horrific portraits of people who have "o.d.'d" (taken a drug overdose): the goal of such presentations seems to be similar to that in aversive conditioning. However, such an approach often does not achieve the desired results. I have worked with several heroin addicts during the past two years who told me they first learned how to shoot up by watching pictures such as these. I recently witnessed a slide presentation in which a close-up of a collapsed jugular vein was shown. The speaker morbidly in-toned, "See what extremes people will go to for a shot of heroin?" Many of the people in the audience gasped in horror, but the young man in front of me whispered to the young woman sitting next to him, "Wild, baby, I never thought you could do it in the neck! I'm gonna try it *that* way next time."

Many students testify that they are impelled to use drugs because they are bored with life. If, instead of spending so much time, effort, and money on drug-education programs, we expended equivalent amounts of energy and funds in facilitating freer exchanges of ideas, information, and experiences among teachers and students, we might do more to reduce boredom (and drug abuse) than we could ever hope to do through formal drug-education programs.

1. Most state departments of education have developed curriculum materials for the public schools. Inquire if your state has such

materials and if they are being used in your local school system. If so, ask the students and teachers how effective they think the program is. Also ask them if they have suggestions for improvement of the program. Take a look at the materials and ask yourself how you would respond to them if you were in high school.

2. If there is no drug-education program in your school or the existing one is inadequate, you might work with both the students and teachers to set up an adequate program. But as an alternative to this approach, make an effort to meet people who are or have been hooked on drugs, and ask them if they would establish a drug-education program if they were given the responsibility. Discuss with physicians, ex-addicts, clergymen and high-school students the pros and cons of establishing a drug-education program in the schools. After these discussions you may come to the conclusion that drug education may be treated most adequately in less formal and less conventional ways.

If you would like to examine some drug-education programs, there are many reputable sources from which you can get them. Here are two good sources.

The National Clearinghouse for Drug Abuse Information has published a series of selected drug-education curricula which are available through the Superintendent of Documents, U.S. Government Printing Office, Washington, D.C. More specific information on these curricula as well as access to a computerized information service for drug abuse can be obtained through writing:

The National Clearinghouse for Drug Abuse Information
Education Services
5454 Wisconsin Avenue
Chevy Chase, Maryland 20015

Some first-rate educational materials have been made available by Roger Conant who has written an interesting and creative comic book entitled, "Who Will Drug You?" and an informative booklet entitled "Be Informed on Drugs." The latter is available for a cost of $.75 through:

New Readers Press
Box 131
Syracuse, New York 13210

Finally, we should remind ourselves that many discussions of drug education are directed only to the needs of young people in the primary and secondary schools. But what about the educational needs of adults as well? Many parents, aunts, and uncles nurture myths and misinformation which, when transmitted to their children, nieces, and nephews, who are often more knowledgeable about drugs, may serve to widen the breach between the generations and make the young people more vulnerable to pressure from their peers who abuse drugs.

VI. CONTINUING EDUCATION COURSES ON DRUGS

1. Many colleges, universities, and continuing education programs throughout the country are offering courses to familiarize community residents about various forms of drug misuse, the different types of treatment modalities, and suggestions for measures to prevent drug misuse. Some of these courses are as long as an academic year or semester (and carry college credit), while others may last for only one or two days (and give no credit). At Cornell University a two-week course is being developed which will be offered during the summer and carries two semester hours of graduate credit.

Although the quality of these courses varies enormously, you may learn a great deal from them. Some states are attempting to coordinate planning of such courses to minimize duplication of offerings and maximize citizen participation. In New York State, for example, several Boards of Cooperative Educational Services have employed Drug Information Coordinators, whose job it is to work with the schools and various public and private agencies in their respective regions to develop and coordinate drug-education courses.

2. If there is no continuing education drug course in the area where you live, discuss the prospect of establishing a course with your local educators, physicians, pharmacists, and clergymen. Often persons who have been addicted to drugs prove to be a great help in developing such a course.

VII. LEGISLATION FOR BETTER PROGRAMS

As Mr. Martin pointed out so eloquently in chapter 4, better legislation and more adequate funding for the rehabilitation programs that legislatures have funded are desperately needed at the federal, state, and municipal levels throughout the country. Some states, such as

Massachusetts, are moving away from a punitive approach to drug addicts to a more enlightened, medically oriented approach. But even in the few states with "model" laws, there is an enormous gap between the wording of the legislation and the appropriations to facilitate the establishment of effective treatment programs.

If your town and state have legislation providing an enlightened approach to drug addiction (and only a small proportion of American cities does), are there provisions for the funds and personnel to implement adequate treatment programs? If not, you may be able to join (or form) a citizens' group to put pressure on your state and federal legislators to pass more adequate laws and provide the appropriations to make these laws workable. You may be surprised to discover how much pressure an effectively organized citizens' group can apply to municipal or state legislative bodies to get better laws and more funds for the treatment of drug abuse.

VIII. PREVALENT SOCIAL ATTITUDES TOWARD DRUG USE

Our society has adopted a whole host of values related to drug use that need to be challenged. We are a nation of people conditioned to the chemical management of our distress and discomfort. We take pills for upset stomachs and headaches, pills if we can't get to sleep, pills to wake us up if we feel sleepy. If we feel "low" or depressed we take stimulants to pep us up, and if we feel too active, we take tranquilizers to calm us.

Millions of American parents—perhaps unwittingly—have transmitted these values of mood alteration through drugs to their children. One manifestation of this process is the widespread use of tranquilizers among many grade-school children. Physicians and teachers have reported that many parents give tranquilizers to their children before they leave for school in the morning with the instructions to take a pill if they feel restless. One teacher in an affluent suburb of Washington, D.C. told me that her sixth-grade students got particularly irritable late in the afternoon because the effects of the tranquilizers taken in the morning had worn off by then.

Testimony given by the Department of Health, Education, and Welfare at a hearing of Congressman Cornelius Gallagher's House Privacy Sub-committee in the fall of 1970 "suggests that 200,000 children in the United States are now being given amphetamine and stimulant therapy, with probably another 100,000 receiving tranquilizers and antidepressants."[1] There is considerable evidence to indicate that the use of drugs by educators and school nurses to modify the behavior of elementary-school children will increase drastically in the coming years unless we take action to reverse this trend.

Another manifestation of warped social values is the widespread use of drugs by children in little-league teams as well as college and professional athletes to improve their performance. A physician who himself placed sixth in the 1968 Olympics decathlon stated that more than a third of the U.S. Olympic team was using drugs during the pre-Olympic training camp. A starting player on Stanford University's Rose Bowl championship team reports that he and many of his teammates used amphetamines for daily practice sessions as well as for games.[2]

This misuse of drugs has been caused by a number of factors in our society. The troika of drug and alcohol manufacturers, advertising agencies, and producers of the mass media have come in for the lion's share of criticism for the uncritical promotion of drug use. Although the strength of isolated individuals in the face of such powerful organizations as these is limited, letters to editors of newspapers and journals and managers of radio and television stations protesting the indiscriminate use of advertisements may have some impact on advertising policy. It is obvious that if you can join (or help form) an organization which is amenable to these goals, the impact of large groups upon manufacturers and advertisers is much greater than the protests of scattered individuals.

Find out if drugs are used in the schools in your community for the modification of behavior of children or for stimulation of better athletic performance. Drugs may be used for these reasons in both grade schools and high schools as well as colleges. If this is so, get your facts clearly documented and bring this matter to the attention of your local P.T.A. or equivalent group—or directly to the board of education. In many cases of this sort, the light of public exposure may bring about radical changes in policy.

---

[1] Charles Witter, "Drugging and Schooling," transaction, July/August, 1971, p. 31.
[2] Jack Scott, "It's Not How You Play the Game, but What Pill You Take," New York Times Magazine, October 17, 1971, pp. 40 ff.

Positively, we must learn to live less superficially. Instead of being obsessed with the desire to use pills to avoid pain and stress, for example, we should learn—in the words of a Yoga instructor—to lean into our pain without taking the pills. By the same token, we should also heighten our ability to derive pleasure from daily living. Sidney Cohen, a psychiatrist who has had extensive experience in treating drug addicts, contends that these people are characterized by anhedonism—the inability to derive pleasure from ordinary experience.[3] If we in our own lives demonstrate the capacity for enjoying simple things, if we show that in spite of the many problems of our communities and the world we can be turned on to life, perhaps that life-style will have an impact on those around us.

CONCLUSION

Finally, it should be pointed out that if all the above recommendations are followed that will solve only part of the drug problem. We may have very adequate and comprehensive programs for working with the millions of Americans who are misusing alcoholic and non-alcoholic drugs. But if at the same time we do not attack the more fundamental social problems contributing to such misuse, we shall be treating only the symptoms of a profoundly crippling malady.

As long as our nation continues to send thousands and thousands of American men to fight in a war they do not support, as long as Whites are pitted against Blacks, as long as our cities become less and less desirable places to live, as long as corrupt police continue to profit from trafficking in narcotics, as long as we pursue with reckless abandon the acquisition of material goods, millions of Americans shall continue to depend on drugs to help them cope with the massive frustrations and anxieties concomitant with these social processes.

Unless we drastically alter the effectiveness with which we deal with these crucial issues—no matter how noble our intentions or sophisticated our programs—we shall fail miserably in our efforts to reach our brothers and our sisters who are misusing drugs.

We must also work to reduce the mass hysteria that is often associated with the misuse of heroin and the hallucinogens. Although the seemingly epidemic spread of addiction to heroin and other related

---

[3] Sidney Cohen, M.D., *The Drug Dilemma* (New York: McGraw-Hill, 1969).

127

drugs is alarming, we should look at this phenomenon in broad perspective.

There is absolutely no question that alcohol and legally prescribed drugs are misused with much greater frequency and in enormously larger quantities than heroin. It has been estimated that for every heroin addict in the United States there are twenty alcoholics. And amphetamine misuse has reached the ranks of persons we do not generally associate with drug abuse. Recently four truck drivers appearing before a Congressional panel estimated that from 75 to 90 percent of all truck drivers "use pep pills and amphetamines at least occasionally to stay awake during long hauls." [4] The widespread misuse of amphetamines and tranquilizers among executives, factory workers, and housewives—groups which we do not associate with the "drug culture"—has been amply documented elsewhere and indicates that honestly confronting drug abuse may require that we minimize the hysteria which in some quarters threatens to engulf us.

In these pages we have suggested a number of programs in which you might become involved and have implied some strategies for effecting social change. But before we launch into new or existing programs, we must be sure that we understand the problem. In the words of Alvin Toffler, "diagnosis precedes cure, and we cannot begin to help ourselves until we become sensitively conscious of the problem." [5]

This book will have achieved its purpose if, in some measure, it has increased your sensitivity to the knotty complex of issues called drug abuse, and stimulated you to translate that sensitivity into your own behavior.

---

[4] *The New York Times,* October 2, 1971, p. 50M.
[5] Alvin Toffler, *Future Shock* (New York: Random House, 1970), p. 417.